The Risk of Relatedness

The Risk of Relatedness

Intersubjectivity Theory in Clinical Practice

Chris Jaenicke

JASON ARONSON
Lanham • Boulder • New York • Toronto • Plymouth, UK

Published in the United States of America
by Jason Aronson
An imprint of Rowman & Littlefield Publishers, Inc.

A wholly owned subsidiary of
The Rowman & Littlefield Publishing Group, Inc.
4501 Forbes Boulevard, Suite 200, Lanham, Maryland 20706
www.rowmanlittlefield.com

Estover Road
Plymouth PL6 7PY
United Kingdom

British Library Cataloguing in Publication Information Available

Library of Congress Cataloging-in-Publication Data

Jaenicke, Chris, 1946–
The risk of relatedness : intersubjectivity theory in clinical practice / Chris Jaenicke.
p. ; cm.
Includes bibliographical references.
ISBN-13: 978-0-7657-0559-4 (cloth)
ISBN-10: 0-7657-0559-1 (cloth)
ISBN-13: 978-0-7657-0560-0 (pbk.)
ISBN-10: 0-7657-0560-5 (pbk.)
1. Psychoanalysis. 2. Psychotherapist and patient. 3. Intersubjectivity. I. Title.
[DNLM: 1. Psychoanalytic Therapy—Case Reports. 2. Professional-Patient Relations—Case Reports. 3. Psychoanalytic Theory—Case Reports. 4. Psychotherapeutic Processes—Case Reports. WM 460.6 J22r 2007]

RC506.J343 2007
616.89'17—dc22 2007022380

O.K., I will walk the line for you,
but don't forget, the line walks you, and us, too.

—C.J.

Contents

Acknowledgments

Writing a book is like going on an expedition. You start by asking some questions but soon find that the answers are pursuing you. You begin by speaking about themes, only to be surprised when they start to talk back to you. Thoughts, once formed, create their own reality. To borrow a metaphor from Stephen King, when you go fishing in the pool, you never know what will wind up in your net. There are some big, hungry ones out there.

It's like our work with our patients: we set out to help them find themselves, and along the way we also discover much about ourselves.

While writing this book I had many companions whom I would like to thank.

Foremost I would like to thank my patients, who invited me into their emotional worlds, opened my eyes, and widened our horizons.

In the early formative psychoanalytic years when I was in training at the National Psychological Association for Psychoanalysis in New York, there were friends and colleagues whose curious and questioning minds helped me through the arduous and often confusing beginnings of becoming an analyst. For their heartfelt support, I would like to thank Lorraine Cates, Alan Dolber, Roberta Galler, Stephen Kurtz, Peter Lessem, Valerie Oltarsch, Jean Owen, and Tom Smith.

The following colleagues read my manuscript or parts of it and contributed valuable ideas and comments: Monika Amler, Hartmut Beucke, Martin Gossmann, Andrea Harms, Frank Horzetzky, Angelika Korp, Joseph Lichtenberg, Donna Orange, Lannie Peyton, and Robert Stolorow.

Donna Orange was the first person—on a rainy walk through Rome—to suggest that I write a book. Her friendship and her work were a constant companion while writing.

Robert Stolorow, mentor, colleague, and friend, has always been an enthusiastic supporter of all levels of my expansiveness.

Crayton Rowe, my first self-psychologically informed supervisor, introduced me to the empathic listening stance and taught me to hear and believe what my patients said.

I would especially like to thank Art Pomponio, editorial director for Jason Aronson Publishers, for giving me the opportunity to publish the book in the country of the language it was originally written in.

I am indebted to my wife, Hilla Jaenicke, for her unflagging enthusiasm, her endurance in accompanying this project, her deep clinical understanding, her encouragement to cast the net in the deep end of the pool, and her belief in me.

Foreword

Robert D. Stolorow, Ph.D.

This is a book about practicing what one's psychoanalytic theory preaches, and it exemplifies this principle better than any other book on therapeutic practice that I have seen to date. Jaenicke's psychoanalytic theory is intersubjective systems theory, a framework that grasps the therapeutic process in terms of understandings acquired in a deep emotional engagement between two people and in the psychological field formed by their interacting emotional worlds. From this theoretical perspective, understanding and emotional engagement constitute an indissoluble contextual whole. Thus, practicing what this theory preaches requires that both participants in the therapeutic process must confront "the risk of relatedness," the emotional red thread that runs through all the chapters of Jaenicke's aptly titled book.

Jaenicke deftly explicates a number of myths that have traditionally been employed by analysts to evade the dangers of emotional engagement—for example, the myth of the neutral and objective analyst and the corresponding myth of uncontaminated transference. Such myths, variants of an overarching doctrine of the isolated mind that psychoanalysis inherited from Descartes, shielded analysts from full awareness of how they were themselves deeply implicated in every aspect of the therapeutic process. What Jaenicke advocates and richly illustrates instead is empathic-introspective investigation of the entire intersubjective system formed by the interacting psychological worlds of both patient and analyst.

Jaenicke shows that at the heart of the shift toward an intersubjective, contextualist perspective in psychoanalysis is the placing of affect—subjective emotional experience—at the center of psychoanalytic theory and practice. Because emotional experience is something that from birth onward takes form within intersubjective contexts, the shift to the motivational primacy of affect contextualizes virtually every aspect of psychoanalytic theory and practice. As Jaenicke illustrates clinically, the contextuality of emotional experience is nowhere seen more vividly than in psychological trauma, grasped as overwhelming, unendurable affect.

Jaenicke suggests forcefully that adopting an intersubjective perspective radically alters one's approach to the analysis of transference, arguably the centerpiece of psychoanalytic method. Transference is understood here as being codetermined by both the patient's psychological world and activities of the analyst that are manifestations of the analyst's psychological world. In their emotional engagement with one another, patient and analyst together constitute a dynamic psychological field, and the essence of psychoanalytic work, in Jaenicke's view, lies in tracking, understanding, and interpretively illuminating the vicissitudes of this complex intersubjective system. His book will be of great help to practitioners in their struggles to confront rather than evade the risks of emotional engagement that such work necessarily entails.

Santa Monica, April 2006

1

Psychoanalytic Myths

> Transference and countertransference together form an intersubjective system of reciprocal mutual influence. Neutral analysts, pure interpretations, uncontaminated transferences—none of these mythological entities can exist within such a system.
>
> (Orange, Atwood, and Stolorow, 1997, p. 40)

> An analyzable patient is a patient with whom the analyst can maintain the illusion of neutrality.
>
> (Gill, 1983, p. 213)

Twenty-five years ago I made a proposal to my training analyst: I asked him to consider our therapeutic process as a game of 52-card pickup. We'd throw all the cards in the air, pick them up, and play them at random. He reacted with consternation and said simply that he couldn't do that. I remember being guided by the wish to encounter him in a new and, for us both, unpredictable way. I felt pressured by an intense longing to break out of my prison of inner isolation and by a diffuse wish that he would become emotionally available to me in a way that hadn't been possible before. His rejection made me redouble my efforts to make contact with him and to be seen in a way that I felt was existential for me. My entire analysis seemed to converge on a single question: feeling like I had just jumped off a cliff, I asked him whether he had the same feelings for me as I had for him. His delphic-analytic answer was that I already knew the answer. That didn't satisfy me, so I plunged ahead and became even more direct. I asked him whether he loved me. I can't remember his answer but it wasn't "yes." Nonetheless he allowed me to see that the posing of the question itself had touched him. He seemed to open a window into himself and let me see something raw and authentic, a mixture of vulnerability, helplessness, awkwardness, and irritation at being pushed so hard. That was enough for me. A gap between my inner self-experience and the gap to him had been closed.

This book has two main topics: the risk of relatedness for both patient and therapist and the clinical application of intersubjective systems theory. I hope to make clear how the two topics are interrelated.

Merton Gill (1983) wrote that "the analyzable patient is a patient with whom the analyst can maintain the illusion of neutrality" (p. 213). In a chapter titled "Beyond Technique," Orange et al. (1997) cite Ferenczi as an important anticipator of their theory of intersubjectivity, having recognized "that psychoanalysis is an intimate human practice" (p. 30). The most general thesis of intersubjectivity theory is that "psychoanalysis seeks to illuminate phenomena that emerge within a specific psychological field constituted by the intersection of two subjectivities—that of the patient and that of the analyst. In this conceptualization, psychoanalysis is not seen as a science of the intrapsychic, focused on events presumed to occur within one isolated 'mental apparatus.'" "Rather, psychoanalysis is pictured here as a science of the *intersubjective*, focused on the interplay between the differently organized subjective worlds of the observer and the observed." "Psychoanalysis is unique among the sciences in that the observer is also the observed" (Atwood and Stolorow, 1984, pp. 41–42).

If the observer is the observed, then there is no longer a "cordon sanitaire" (Brandchaft, 1993) around the therapist. This increases the risk of relatedness immeasurably for the therapist and puts him in a much more vulnerable position. Therapists have always been exposed to the tumultuous feelings of their patients. However, if pathology is no longer viewed as located solely within the patient and if the patient's affective states are viewed as part and parcel of the psychoanalytic field being investigated, a field that is codetermined not only by the therapist's reactions and effect on the patient but also by the very fabric of his or her personality, then we begin to understand the risk of relatedness to both participants and the potential need for both to react defensively—the patient by viewing the therapist as a detached professional and the therapist by detaching himself by seeing the patient as pathological.

I offered the clinical vignette of my training analysis not so much as an insight into my psyche, although I'm sure conclusions could be drawn, but rather to exemplify three main theses of this book. The first is that from an intersubjective viewpoint, the risk of relatedness is an inherent and necessary part of therapeutic treatment insofar as mutual regulation is seen as a sine qua non of the therapeutic process. The second point I wish to make is that the choice of psychoanalytic or therapeutic school a clinician adheres to is closely related to his or her subjectivity, just as all theories are grounded in the subjectivity of the theorists (Atwood and Stolorow, 1979). Third, not only can no one escape their subjectivity in treatment, but it must also be seen as the basis from which we do our work.

THE MYTH OF THE ISOLATED MIND

Following this line of argumentation and in order to give the reader an orientation into the world of intersubjectivity, it would be helpful to describe some of the basic tenets of the intersubjective philosophy of life. To put it imagistically, everything hangs from a thread. Everything is interdependent—our well-being and our ill-being—hence, everything is potentially our salvation and our undoing. We are always potentially at risk. The two sides of the coin of intersubjectivity are connectedness and the failure to connect—to ourselves, each other, and the world. At the same time, we are always part of an intersubjective field; both connectedness and disconnectedness are a function of the fields we find ourselves in and those that were relationally constitutional for us. Because we view human existance as totally dependent on our ability to be connected to our own subjectivity, to the surround, to nature, and to others, there is one part of us that is basically petrified about being alive. We know we will die, we fear being failed or left by others, and we even know that the very experience of reality and the permanance of the world are a product of our experiences of embeddedness. Hence, Orange et al.'s (1997) term of the *unbearable embeddedness of being*. Subjectively, the denial or loss of our sense of embeddedness can lead to the dissolution of our sense of self-experience or our sense of an existing reality. The idea that an objective reality exists apart from our subjective experience is another variation of the illusion that we can exist without all of that which sustains us. In order to combat these existential vulnerabilities, we have created the myth of the isolated mind, the myth of an autonomous self-sufficiency. We understand this myth to be pervasive in Western industrial culture and society. We view this myth as a form of defensive grandiosity whose function it is to ward off the abyss—in terms of our vulnerability—that we all feel we're hanging over.

In psychoanalysis, this defensive grandiosity has led to theories believing in various reifications of mental processes that are presumed to occur within the individual person—in Freudian theory to a mental apparatus driven by endogenous drives, in ego psychology to an autonomously self-regulating ego, and in self psychology to a reified vision of a self with a preordained nuclear design. Orange et al. have argued that "the pervasive, reified image of the mind in isolation . . . is a form of defensive grandiosity that serves to disavow the exquisite vulnerability that is inherent to an awareness of the embeddedness of all human experience in constitutive relational systems" (Orange et al., 1997, p. 42). The central myth of the isolated psyche has spawned a number of other myths: the myth of neutrality, with the closely related issues of neutrality as abstinence, as anonymity, and as the analyst maintaining a stance that is equidistant from the id, the ego, and the superego. In self psychology, analytic neutrality has also been equated with empathy. The myth of interpretation without suggestion, the myth of uncontaminated transference, and the myth of objectivity are further fictions underlying the traditional analytic stance. Central to this chapter is the myth that the therapist is not deeply implicated in the process of treatment and in the domain that, in our view, defines the object of psychoanalytic scrutiny: the intersubjective field of the therapeutic dyad, which is itself embedded in a multitude of intersubjective worlds.

THE MYTH OF NEUTRALITY

"The ideal of the neutral and objective analyst, impenetrable and sagelike, is just such an image (of the isolated mind) in that it disavows the deeply personal impact of the analyst's emotional engagement with patients and denies all the ways in which the analyst and his or her own psychological organization are profoundly implicated in all the phenomena he or she observes and seeks to treat. In order to dispense with the defensive invincibility and omniscience of the neutral stance, analysts must be prepared to bear the profound feelings of vulnerability and anxious uncertainty that are inevitable accompaniments in a deep analytic process. Letting go of metapsychological and epistemological absolutes and the security of standardized technique exposes analysts to the necessity of confronting 'Cartesian anxiety' (Bernstein, 1983)—their 'dread of structureless chaos'" (Stolorow, Atwood, and Brandchaft, 1994, cited in Orange et al., 1997, p. 42). The myth of objectivity denies the indivisibility of the observer and the observed in psychoanalysis as well as the coconstructed nature of analytic truth.

From an intersubjectivist point of view, the myth of the isolated mind serves to mask a profound sense of aloneness so entrenched it escapes our notice. Instead, it is as much taken as a given as our ingrained feeling that we basically have to master our life on our own, somewhat reminiscent of an old saying from the 1970s: "I've been down so long, it looks like up to me." The question arises again what function is served by this objectivistic epistemology, which sees the mind in isolation, "radically separated from an external reality that it either accurately apprehends or distorts" (Orange et al., 1997, p. 41). We feel that a mind looking out on an external world is much like a knight who looks through the slit of his visor and is a heroic image or myth. Being disconnected from all that sustains life, it follows that it takes heroic efforts to conquer life. In psychoanalysis, it then becomes the heroic task of beknighted therapists who adhere to this doctrine to assess and reorder the pathological processes occurring solely within an individual. What makes the radical separation, the heroic view, necessary? Besides the defensive function of warding off feelings of vulnerability, it is my contention that we, analogous to our patients, if not necessarily on the same structural level, feel threatened by being touched and changed. But there is more: if therapist and patient, observer and observed, form an indissoluble unit in terms of mutual regulation, then there is no escaping the fields we find ourselves in. While this in and of itself does not mean that we necessarily experience ourselves as especially close and similar to (or distant and distinct from) our patients, it does preclude the possible escape into the stance of neutrality: robbed of the perch of our neutral observation post from which we assess the distorted transferences of our patients, we may experience the reciprocal mutual influence of the analytic exchange as feelings of lostness, disorientation, and fear. In some of our analytic work, the water gets so deep that we may feel we lose sight of the bottom and the shore. For myself and my work with supervisees, I have found it necessary and helpful to acknowledge feeling threatened by some of our therapeutic engagements. At the same time, there's a natural resistance to acknowledging such limitations, as it seems to question our task and the ability to be responsible for our patients. "Therapists are especially prone to make claims of neutrality when their patients' transference attributions threaten essential features of their sense of self" (Orange et al., 1997, p. 36).

Schwaber (1983) put it this way: "It was that I felt a particular resistance to being experienced in this way, as central to another's experience, while so different from how I felt myself to be . . . a resistance to the acknowledgment that the truth we believe about ourselves is no more (though no less) 'real' than the patient's view of us—that all we can 'know' about ourselves is our own psychic reality" (p. 389). A critique may be made along the lines that "if you can't stand the heat, then don't go in the kitchen," or is this view of our work an overdramatization? The counterargument is that it is a collective taboo, based on the pervasive heroic myth of the invincibility of the isolated mind, to avoid public discussions of feelings of weakness in regard to our work.

Returning to the case vignette with my training analyst as an example of the heat of the analytic kitchen, I will fantasize a number of his possible reactions. While being able to hold my intense idealizing transference is a frequent enough bread-and-butter analytic task, one that demands that he be able to remain an elusive presence allowing the unfolding of my inner world, he may have felt uncomfortable at my claim to having or wanting such a central role in his life. The question of love may have been experienced as overstepping his personal boundaries or may have stimulated any number of other issues. For me, I may have experienced his very calmness as a repeat of being ignored in the past. In the end, it was neither the subjective truth of my need to be lovable nor his need to be true to remaining delineated and authentic that counted. Instead, we arrived at a truth that was truthful for our particular intersubjective field. For this to occur, both had to allow the process of mutual regulation to move us. In this sense, we did play 52-card pickup. The image of 52-card pickup can be understood as an attempt to break free of the rigid mold of the monadic mind.

Before continuing the discussion of the myth of the isolated mind and those psychoanalytic concepts that are closely related to the issue of excluding the analyst's subjectivity from the therapeutic process, it is necessary to examine a recurring misunderstanding about intersubjectivity theory. This misunderstanding is based on the fear of *anarchy* in the analytic relationship (Stolorow et al., 1994). Here the parity ascribed to the worlds of patient and analyst on the level of mutual regulation as well as "at the level of abstract conceptualization of the therapeutic dyad becomes, however, misinterpreted as implying *symmetry* in that relationship at the level of concrete clinical practice" (Stolorow et al., 1994, p. 209). The central idea of interacting subjective worlds becomes misinterpreted as a giving up of the distinction between patient and analyst. The fact that the subjectivity of the analyst is always implicated in our attempts to understand the patient has led to the question, Whose analysis is this, anyway? To clarify: intersubjectivity theory believes, in accordance with Aron's (1996) view, that the analyst is a "co-participant involved in a mutual if *asymmetrical* endeavor" (p. 258). This in no way implies a confusion of who is the patient and who is the analyst, nor does it imply that the analyst gives up the responsibility for the process and the conditions of the treatment. The image of an analytic interaction being described as a game of 52-card pickup addresses the idea of mutuality in attempting to understand the exchange; it does not suggest the giving up of the analayst's role in terms of remaining focused on the unfolding, illumination, interpretation, and transformation of the patient's subjective world. The fact that such an understanding of the analytic relationship may be *experienced* by analysts as anarchy has more to do with fears connected to understanding that we can't hide behind our role in terms of the impact we have on patients and that they have on us than with meaning that we should give up or are in danger of losing our role. Now let us imagine the analyst or therapist as he or she steps into seven or eight intersubjective fields each day. In each, the analyst must accommodate and assimilate according to the demands of each unique person and each particular field. It is for this reason that I speak of the risk of relatedness involved in our profession. Martin Bergmann once said that he was always a little bit afraid when he picked up his patients in the waiting room. There is a truism from the blues that says, "If you ain't scared, you ain't right." Entering into the intersubjective field, a therapist has to be willing to hold, modulate, and be responsive to the various types of strong emotions—or to profound disconnectedness of affect—of his or her patients. This may entail, in turn, being the recipient of hours of mistrust, months or years of the patient's disbelief in the possibility of positive change, long stretches of time of not understanding what is happening in the treatment, the necessity of keeping gestalts open until understanding emerges between the participants, and allowing and holding such strong emotions as despondency, rage, idealization, and the love of patients. This places a high demand on the analyst's emotional availability (Orange, 1995) as well as an understanding of his or her vacillations in availability and an attitude of fallibility: that we don't understand at least as much as that we do and that understanding is a task that demands a degree of flexibility that at times puts a tremendous strain on our own need to maintain our subjective organization. In other words, we also need to hold, modulate, and be attuned to our own affects while trying to ascertain their impact on the patient. Perhaps we can understand the origins and the necessity of the concepts of the isolated mind and neutrality as we become more able to acknowledge the centrality of affectivity for ourselves and psychotherapeutic treatment. Perhaps this explains a certain blindness in psychoanalysis: to believe that we could be involved in deep processes of transformation without being transformed ourselves. To allow ourselves to be emotionally touched and to touch is probably just as often disturbing as it is exhilarating. We are constantly either avoiding or inviting it, revealing ourselves or hiding. Being in resonance with our patients (or avoiding it) is an inherent part of therapy. This silent aspect of our work entails a major part of our therapeutic task. For the patient, it has curative functions; for the therapist, it explains the demanding nature of our work.

In their first book, *Faces in a Cloud,* Atwood and Stolorow (1979) demonstrated by means of four psychobiographical case studies of major psychoanalytic theorists (Freud, Jung, Reich, and Rank) how closely the subjective worlds of the theorists were linked to their main "metapsychological conceptions and hypotheses regarding human nature" (p. 5) and how this limits the generality of their theoretical constructions. They therefore came to the conclusion that a theory of subjectivity itself was needed. Eventually, the theory of intersubjectivity evolved from this insight, one main point being that it was neither possible nor necessary to attempt to exclude the subjectivity of the analyst from the psychoanalytic process. On the contrary, a theory was needed that allows for the inevitable impact of the subjectivity of the therapist. From this vantage point, it becomes fascinating to examine the subjective nature of some of the most central concepts of psychoanalysis, all of which seem to be geared to eliminating the intersubjective factor. The following description of the concept of neutrality is based extensively on Orange et al.'s (1997) work, as it is central to understanding how and where the traditional analytic stance differs from the intersubjective stance.

THE MYTH OF NEUTRALITY AS ABSTINENCE

Let me begin with the concept of neutrality as abstinence and Freud's (1915a) dictum that the therapeutic process should be carried out in abstinence, a concept that, it is well known, he himself did not necessarily adhere to. Nonetheless, it has successfully terrorized generations of analytic candidates. As one candidate put it, "During all of our training the club of neutrality has been hanging over us." The idea was to deny patients any form of instinctual gratification because, otherwise, repressed instinctual wishes could not become conscious. They would be acted out by therapist and patient, and therefore their symbolization couldn't take place, the genetic origins couldn't be examined, and ultimately infantile wishes would not be sublimated or given up. Most likely, Freud was also guided by the criticism of psychoanalysis in his time, fearing that untoward events were taking place on the couch. Abstinence, however, can hardly be viewed as neutral because it is based on specific assumptions about "human nature, motivation, maturity and psychological illness and health" (Orange et al., 1997, p. 36). In other words, as pointed out previously, the concept expresses a "deeply held belief system" (p. 36) and originates in the subjectivity of the theorist. The issue here is not so much the theory itself, although from the standpoint of developmental psychology much can and will be said about developmental needs of patients and how to respond to them. The point is simply that it is not without subjectivity. It needs to be said that anyone can work intersubjectively as long as he or she is aware of how one's interventions and treatment approach are guided by one's subjectivity, including the theory that informs the practitioner, and as long as the therapist is alert to how a particular patient responds to each theory-guided intervention. This should also not be misunderstood as a plea for theory-free treatment, as that would be as impossible as trying to banish the therapist's subjectivity; rather, each theory has subjective origins that delimit its generality and validity (Stolorow, Brandchaft, and Atwood, 1987).

From the perspective of the patient, the consistent frustration of his or her needs and wishes will not be experienced as neutral. In fact, it may lead to anger and conflict. If this is then interpreted as being part of the patient's pathology, we are adding insult to injury. "As Stone (1961) and Gill (1984) have pointed out, so-called regressive transference neuroses, thought by many to be the sine qua non of an analytic process, may actually be iatrogenic reactions to the indiscriminate application of the principle of abstinence" (Orange et al., 1997, p. 36).

Another dimension of analytic neutrality concerns Freud's (1912) recommendation that the analyst "should be opaque to his patients and, like a mirror, should show them nothing but what is shown to him" (p. 118). This is another aspect of neutrality that is still pervasive in analytic training as an important part of the traditional analytic stance. It entails the idea that therapists could actually exclude their personalities from the therapeutic dialogue, whereas we influence the process through every fiber of our being as it is expressed verbally and nonverbally to our patients. To believe that our patients are not gathering or on some level taking in consciously or unconsciously every bit of information that we expose them to is to once again deny the intersubjective nature of the therapeutic exchange. In an analogous manner, infant research has taught us how humans influence each other's behavior in fractions of seconds. As therapists, we show ourselves in the way we furnish our practices, in the way we dress, in the cadences of our voices, in the expressions on our faces, and with every utterance we make. "Everything the analyst does or says—including especially the interpretations offered—are products of his or her psychological organization, disclosing *central aspects of the anaylst's personality to the patient*" (Orange et al., 1997, p. 37, emphasis added). One ecologically minded patient of mine felt threatened in his ability to idealize me by the fact that I had a Coke can on my table. Other patients became doubtful about my abilities because I had glossy magazines describing the fates of the rich and famous in my waiting room, while others found this not to be culturally substandard but rather a sign of my liberalness.

At this point, it is necessary to differentiate between Orange et al.'s (1997) concept of intersubjectivity and that of Stern (1985). "Intersubjectivity theory intends to describe the emergence and modification of subjectivity, and defines *these processes as irreducibly relational*" (Orange et al., 1997, p. 4, emphasis added). It does not "refer primarily to a developmental achievement" as noted in Stern (1985); rather, it is seen "as a stage and process of recognition of another's subjectivity as connected and responsive to one's own" (Orange et al., 1997, p. 4). In other words, we need to distinguish between a patient's ability to recognize us in our subjectivity and the idea that our subjectivity will nonetheless always be implicated in our patients' reactions to us. An obvious example would be a patient not recognizing the fact that his or her therapist is pregnant. As Jaenicke and Milch (2002) have noted elsewhere, "The task of the analyst is not to focus on a quixotic battle against his or her own subjectivity, but rather to constantly attempt to understand how the patient has unconsciously or consciously processed the analytic relationship" (p. 265). From an intersubjective viewpoint, the impressions that our patients have of us are "decisive in co-determining the development of the transference" (Orange et al., 1997, p. 37). It follows that a therapist's mistaken belief that he or she can cleanse the therapeutic dialogue of their personality will also have an effect on the transference that will need to be taken into account.

THE MYTH OF NEUTRALITY AS OBJECTIVITY

Another concept of neutrality is based on Anna Freud's (1936) idea of an analytic stance that is "equidistant from the id, the ego and the super-ego" (p. 28), a stance that she equates with "clear objectivity" and an "absence of bias" (pp. 28–29). As Orange et al. (1997) point out, this concept of neutrality is based on the tripartite model of the mind—"a value-laden theoretical belief system" (p. 37) that therefore cannot be regarded as unbiased or neutral. Interpretations that are made on this model of the mind must be seen as part of the analyst's belief system, and, to the extent that the patient is encouraged to adopt this particular viewpoint, they are suggestions. This is not to say that our interpretations should be theory-free; on the contrary, they must be seen as part of the subjectivity we offer to the patient and must therefore be assessed as to how the patient organizes this aspect of our personalities. Obviously, this applies to those therapists whose work is informed by intersubjectivity theory as well. The objection applies to the notion, once again, of neutrality.

Self psychology has also not been exempt from the myth of neutrality. Kohut (1977) defined analytic neutrality "as the responsiveness to be expected, on an average, from persons who have devoted their life to helping others with the aid of insights obtained via empathic immersion into their inner life" (p. 252). This stance is also rooted in a theoretical belief system, one that accentuates the importance of emotional responsiveness. Kohut (1980) himself understood that patients will not experience prolonged empathic immersion on the part of the therapist as neutral insofar as it meets the profound need to be understood (Orange et al., 1997). Indeed, the clinical *effect* of empathy has often not been sufficiently understood and is discussed in the next chapter. Nonetheless, Kohut (1980) thought that empathy "is in essence neutral and objective" (p. 483). Once again, to expect a therapist to be able to view his or her patients from a neutral perspective would mean that he or she could see the patient through a "God's-eye view" (Orange, 1995) rather than through the lens of his or her own subjectivity.

THE MYTH OF NEUTRALITY AND MUTUAL REGULATION

The thorough examination of neutrality and its clinical offshoots was intended to show its centrality for the traditional analytic stance and to illustrate where and how intersubjectivity theory differs from the traditional view. This could be understood as an abandoning of some of the analyst's most cherished beliefs or as an act of disloyalty to Freud. I hope to dispel this notion insofar as I feel indebted to the founder of psychoanalysis in the sense that Stephan Mitchell expressed it: Freud has the first word on most psychoanalytic topics but not the last. On the contrary, I view the further development of his revolutionary ideas to be in the spirit of Freud. It is my intention not to denigrate the work of traditional psychoanalysts but to demonstrate that psychoanalysis is a vital science in a process of constant development. As a result, some psychoanalytic concepts have become anachronistic. I would like to show that a failure to acknowledge these changes places unnecessary restraints on the patient, the analyst, and the therapeutic process itself. One of the reasons we have difficulties in embracing developments is because we are our own instruments and because our theories are so intricately interwoven with our subjectivities. Therefore, we may experience new ideas as a personal attack. A related, understandable explanation may be found in the passion with which we attempt to defend, maintain, and live by our own theories. My purpose is to offer an empathic explanation of why we have had such difficulty in transcending the concept of neutrality. The main hindrance seems to be, in my opinion, the notion of mutual regulation. Mutual regulation is a concept that is perhaps understandable enough, but to live and work with it is an entirely different matter. The walls of our monadic castles can be formidably high. To this day, I find myself scampering for their safety.

If it is true that all theories are based on belief systems, then this will also apply to the following description of the human condition with which I would like to introduce my explanation. At any age or stage or in any situation, it is a risk to open ourselves to another human being. Because none of us has escaped being hurt and because we know the risk involved in allowing ourselves to be emotionally touched, we try to minimize that risk, all the while forgetting what the cost is of shutting others out, in the extreme, to becoming isolated. The myth of the isolated mind is the last bastion in our attempt to defend ourselves against pain. The corollary myth of neutrality is a prime example of trying to uphold the idea that there isn't always mutuality in the human exchange.

To put it in Kohut's (1984) words,

> Man of our time is the man of the precariously cohesive self, the man who craves the presence, the interest, the availability of the self-cohesion–maintaining selfobject. It is the very intensity of this need that via a wall of secondary prideful disavowal accounts for the fact that he may experience our theory that the self's autonomy is only relative, that, in principle, a self can never exist outside a matrix of selfobjects, as a serious narcissistic blow. (p. 61)

In the past, psychoanalysis claimed that neutrality was an attempt to avoid undue influence on the patient—by being anonymous, objective, abstinent, or empathic—in order not to contaminate or block the patient's unfolding transference or his or her development in general. But perhaps there is another purpose that is equally taboo: analysts fearing the consequences of allowing themselves to develop by accepting that reciprocal mutuality is truly a two-way street—in terms of intersubjective systems theory, by accepting the intersubjective fields that we live in and that determine the nature of the analytic exchange.

The concept of neutrality therefore seems to serve dual purposes, both of which have to do with avoiding the perils of contact. For one, it distances us from taking responsibility for our impact on patients. On a macroscopic level, being implicated in our patients' reactions means that pathology can no longer be seen as located solely in the patient but also—as it arises and recedes in the therapeutic process—as a product of the intersubjective field. The idea that we are implicated in our patients' pathology is too close to home, experientially akin to having someone severely psychologically ill in the family. On a microscopic level, it means that everything we are and do, especially our interpretations, is implicit in our patients' reactions. This can easily be observed in a close examination of protocols of therapeutic sessions. Looking at patients' responses to our interventions mercilessly demonstrates whether we have furthered, blocked, or derailed the unfolding of the patient's inner world. Patients are very patient with us in that they often just ignore what we have said and continue in their agenda. But just as often, we can see how they feel obliged to accommodate us and sustain the sense of *our* subjectivity, albeit in order not to threaten the vitally needed tie to us.

Not only does this greatly increase the weight of our responsibility toward our patients, but it can also be deeply unsettling to our view of ourselves, as the foundations of our subjectivity may be shaken. If we accept the microscopic impact we have on patients, then we have to constantly be self-reflective in order to gauge the impact of our subjective views or, as Gadamer (1990) put it, of our prejudices. We have to be prepared to decenter from our perspective in order to achieve an approximate understanding of the patient. Wearing the coats of our theories lightly (Orange, 1995), relativizing our subjective viewpoints in order to understand analytic truth as an emergent product of both subjectivities, demands a nimbleness of psychological footing that can be potentially destabilizing. Attempting to consistently understand the perspective of the other can be experienced as distancing from ourselves. One colleague humorously put it this way: "If I were to constantly work self-psychologically, I'd go crazy." Insofar as we are identified with our professional selves, as many of us are (which also explains the passion of our theoretical disputes), our work constantly demands that we are willing to doubt ourselves. In time, we learn to live with open questions, stumbling in the dark in regard to our patients. Nonetheless, this professional uncertainty takes its toll because of the inextricable involvement of our subjectivity. To summarize the first purpose of neutrality, to ward off feelings of inadequacy and insecurity toward our patients, we demand invincibility and omniscience of ourselves and clothe it in the armor of the heroic myth of the isolated mind. Neutrality is understood as a denial of our subjective impact on patients.

The second purpose pertains to our denial of the patient's impact on us. This is a very ticklish question for psychotherapists, as it involves a number of taboos that, on examination, once again revolve around the subjectivity of the therapist. Searles (1965) was one the first analysts to have bravely written about this issue. In his *Collected Papers on Schizophrenia and Related Subjects,* he describes what can be entailed in the very deep work with patients suffering from psychosis. He wrote how the very foundations of his life were put into question—his professional abilities as well as his most intimate relationships. It seems like a truism to postulate that if we are to be able to resonate with the deepest emotions of our patients, then our own deepest feelings will be called forth. Not every analyst will be able to resonate with each particular patient's affect. In fact, we assess analyzability not on the basis of a patient's pathology but rather as an intersubjective phenomenon of the patient–analyst fit. In other words, our ability to treat someone depends on our emotional availability toward a unique individual. The seeming strangeness and lack of boundaries that is encoded in a psychotic worldview may be experienced as too threatening to our commonly held beliefs or our own sense of subjectivity. To varying degrees, any kind of deep psychotherapeutic process will confront us with our deepest affects. To clarify, I am not saying that one has to have an enfeebled, porous sense of self or be extremely needy to work with archaic states. That would be to romanticize the experiential horrors of psychological illness and a variation of the theme of linking genius with insanity. I am saying that areas of enfeeblement and neediness will go into resonance with the patient. The pretension that we are without needs or that we are paragons of health is another mythological dragon in need of slaying. We are dependent on our patients not only for our livelihood but also, in allowing us to help them, for giving our lives meaning. Thus, two basic human needs, in my opinion, are met (or not) through our work: our sense of efficacy in the world and our sense of having meaning. This makes it difficult to describe us as neutral participants.

Defining the therapeutic process as mutual but asymmetric means that we have to allow ourselves to be drawn into deep processes while maintaining the focus on the patient. It seems like a paradoxical demand to allow and acknowledge the full involvement of our subjectivity while constantly reflecting and decentering from it at the same time. So we have to be able to be affected by our patients but not so much that we lose sight of the therapeutic endeavor. This is easier said than done when, for instance, feelings of rage, loving feelings, devalued feelings, sexual feelings, moments of losing boundaries or felt threats to our cohesion, or feelings of profound professional failure occur. You can't swim without getting wet, and to move our patients, we have to allow ourselves to be moved. To a certain degree, we have to allow ourselves to become destabilized in order to reorganize on a higher level. It is not only the patient's system that undergoes destabilization in order to reorganize on a more inclusive systems level.

On the one hand, we need to be watchful not to confuse the prerequisite to maintain asymmetry and uphold our therapeutic role with a misguided idea of neutrality, which is, in fact, a defense against involvement in the therapeutic process. On the other hand, we need to be aware that the necessity of relatedness also entails the risks of relatedness by admitting that our work can be dangerous. Thus, while it is not hard to empathize with the felt necessity of a neutral stance, as any kind of defensiveness must be understood in terms of subjective danger, it also has been a crushing weight on generations of analytic candidates who do not feel free to speak of their deeply felt fears in connection to not living up to this ideal. "The myth of neutrality has been destructive insofar as it has hindered analysts from a guilt-free usage of the idiosyncratic wealth of their personalities and has instead tied them into a virtual corset of ideal analytic behavior" (Jaenicke and Milch, 2002, p. 265). Trainees live in constant terror of not behaving analytically, and some of their best interventions are lost to their patients even as they are expressed to their supervisors.

Before turning to the alternative to neutrality in the next chapter—the stance of empathic-introspective inquiry and the concept of empathy—it is important to emphasize that our stance is "neither meant as a prescription for deliberate self-disclosure nor an advocation of a particular form of emotional responsiveness on the part of the analyst. It does not question the asymmetry of the analytic relationship, a non-directive attitude or the distinction between an analytic and a problem-solving therapeutic approach, although as with any analytic behavior, the effect on the patient [of this stance] has to be understood. Instead the focus is on the inner world of the patient and the interplay with the constitutive intersubjective field as he or she experiences it" (Jaenicke and Milch, 2002, p. 265).

Intersubjectivity theory does not mitigate the importance of intrapsychic phenomena. It does insist, however, on the contextualization of inner processes.

THE MYTH OF THE SUGGESTION-FREE INTERPRETATION

Three other myths that are closely related to the myth of the neutral analyst have been influential in determining the traditional analytic stance (Orange et al., 1997). One of the trademarks of psychoanalysis in contrast to other forms of psychotherapy has been the interpretation of transference as oppposed to suggestion. This differentiation between interpretation and suggestion is closely related to the concept of neutrality in that it implies that an analyst is able to offer interpretations without suggestion. The idea that transference interpretations, if properly executed, reflect only what is unconscious in the patient fails to take into account that every interpretation involves a decision of the analyst in terms of the material he or she has chosen to address. In this sense, it invites the patient to follow the direction of the analyst and to see things, if minutely, from the perspective of the analyst. In other words, it fails to take the subjectivity of the analyst, which in turn is rooted in a theoretical framework and entwined with his or her deeply felt value system, into account in the framing of interpretations. "Thus every interpretation that is offered will be colored, in varying degrees, by the analyst's own perspective. To that extent, interpretations are suggestions" (Jaenicke, 2002, p. 208). Once again, it is critical to assess whether the patient feels obliged to adapt to the analyst's view in order to safeguard the bond.

THE MYTH OF THE UNCONTAMINATED TRANSFERENCE

The myth of the uncontaminated transference is based on the assumption that a neutral analyst can refrain from "contaminating" the transference through his or her subjectivity and thus enable the patient to displace in pure culture "emotions belonging to an unconscious representation of a repressed object to a mental representation of an object in the external world" (Nunberg, 1951, p. 1, cited in Orange et al., 1997, p. 39). This view of transference as displacement assumes that the patient's experience of the analyst is solely a product of his or past and psychopathology. It neglects the fact that transference is codetermined by the analyst's contributions and the structures of meaning into which these are assimilated by the patient. Consistent with the concept of mutual regulation, transference will always be evoked by some quality or activity of the analyst that lends itself to being assimilated into developmentally preformed organizing principles. The concept of transference as an unconscious organizing principle as opposed to displacement, regression, projection, or distortion will be taken up in detail in a following chapter. Countertransference is also conceptualized broadly as a manifestation of the analyst's unconscious organizing principles and as being decisive in shaping the patient's transference. Transference and countertransference therefore form an intersubjective system of reciprocal mutual influence (Stolorow et al., 1987). "Neutral analysts, pure interpretations, uncontaminated transferences—none of these mythological entities can exist within such a system" (Orange et al., 1997, p. 40).

THE MYTH OF OBJECTIVITY

The third myth that is entwined with the notion of the neutral analyst is the myth of objectivity. Here the image of the analyst as a natural scientist making objective observations about the patient, especially the transference, is evoked. This brings to mind the many associations that patients have had of analysts as scientists in white laboratory coats or as dentists. Having myself described as a dentist always makes me question what I have said or done that might lend itself to the patient's feeling penetrated in a painful, mechanical way and invites me to think about whether I have felt a need to distance myself from the patient. Or have I, slipping into an objectivist epistemology, given the patient to understand that I possess the God's-eye view of his or her true reality that his or her transference experience has distorted? In patients who have suffered from extreme experiences of having their perceptions doubted, this can lead to feelings of annihilation. In contrast, some interpretations of empathy have led analysts to claim that they are able to make direct empathic contact with the patient's reality by having access to the patient's subjectivity via vicarious introspection. In both cases, the assumption is that the analyst can make observations that are not unconsciously shaped by their subjectivity. "This myth of objectivity denies the essential indivisibility of the observer and the observed in psychoanalysis, as well as the coconstructed *nature of analytic truth*" (Orange et al., 1997, p. 41, emphasis added). From an intersubjective, perspectivalist view, the analyst's perceptions are not more true than the patient's. Because we cannot directly know the psychic reality of the patient, we can arrive at only an approximation of the patient's psychic reality as it is filtered through the lens of our own subjectivity. This means that analytic truth is an emergent property of the dialogue between the two participants. The fact that we view the "truth" as emerging may be experienced by some analysts as a threat to their sense of competence or authority, as it again illustrates the vulnerability inherent in giving up the notion of the heroic isolated mind. As noted earlier, analyzability then is no longer the property of the patient alone, dictated by the "objective" assessment of the analyst, but rather a result of assessing the functioning of the system. The question then is, How good or bad is the fit between each unique therapeutic dyad?

2

Empathic-Introspective Inquiry: An Intersubjective Alternative to Neutrality

> Empathy, I believe, is emotional knowledge gained by participating in a shared reality.
>
> (Donna Orange)

> The quality of understanding is personally endured.
>
> (Dina Vallino Maccio)

If we give up the analytic stance of neutrality, abandoning the safe harbor of anonymity, objectivity, and abstinence, how can we conceptualize the process of understanding the patient? Stolorow, Brandchaft, and Atwood (1987) "have characterized this stance as one of empathic-introspective inquiry. Such inquiry seeks to illuminate the principles unconsciously organizing the patient's experience (empathy), the principles unconsciously organizing the analyst's experience (introspection) and the oscillating psychological field created by the interplay between the two (intersubjectivity)" (Orange, Atwood, and Stolorow, 1997, pp. 43–44).

To understand this stance, we need to go back further in time to Kohut's revolutionary introduction of empathy into psychoanalysis (Kohut, 1959). John Gedo (1975) wrote that he thought this article to be the most important Kohut ever wrote, adding that it's difficult for others to imagine how radical and unacceptable his ideas were for the psychoanalytic community of his time. The following discussion of the concept of empathy will raise the question of to what degree this is still true. The concept of empathy is as complex as it was decisive in altering the course of psychoanalysis. Nonetheless, it has been often misunderstood and brushed aside. Introspection and empathy are also central concepts—with the exception of not being viewed as a "value-neutral mode of observation" (p. 84)—in intersubjectivity theory. For these reasons, it is necessary to examine them in some detail.

Kohut's main thesis is that the method of observation, that is, the way we listen to our patients, not only determines the relationship between analyst and patient but also delimits and defines psychoanalysis. In his second paper on empathy, written and presented shortly before his death, Kohut (1982) began with the main themes of his 1959 paper. By then, he was quite weary of explaining this concept but, because of its centrality, felt obliged to do so once again. The word *empathy* itself seems to be predestined to be misunderstood, as it seems for some ears to this day to connote a touchy-feely attitude rather than the scientific rigor with which Kohut used it. This may be why he began explaining empathy by stating what it is not:

> I did not write about empathy as associated with any specific *emotion* such as, in particular, *compassion or affection*. It may be motivated by, and used in the service of, *hostile or destructive aims*. I did not write about empathy as associated with intuition. As is the case with extrospection, it may, occasionally, be used seemingly intuitively by experts: that is, via mental processes of observation that identify complex configurations preconsciously and at great speed. But mostly, certainly in psychoanalysis, empathy is used non-intuitively, ploddingly, if you wish, by trial and error. I did not write about empathy as being always correct and accurate. . . . We must . . . be able to tolerate uncertainty and to postpone our closures. (Kohut, 1984b, p. 83, emphasis added)

Here Kohut is writing about empathy as "a mode of observation attuned to the inner life of man, just as extrospection is a mode of observation attuned to the external world" (p. 84). He is writing about empathy as an information-collecting, data-gathering activity, as experience-near theory. He differentiates between the high and low road in science, no value judgment implied. The low road is the empirical stance, the high road the epistemological. The epistemological stance examines the relationship between the data that have already been collected and the experience-near theories that have already been deduced. Kohut believed both to be necessary. In fact, it was his knowledge of the failure of his experience-distant theories in his clinical work that led him to a reexamination of his experience-near mode of observation. Like in every science, he believed in the value of experience-distant theories to provide the framework for the pragmatic work and that from time to time "we should move from the low road of pragmatism to the high road of epistemology—only to return to the first in order to test the new theoretical vantage point that we now may have adopted" (p. 84).

Before we can focus our attention on the low road of pragmatism, the clinical application and clinical effect of the empathic-introspective stance, it will be necessary to explore the high road of epistemology further and try to understand why Kohut (1984) felt impelled "to undertake an epistemological investigation concerning the quintessence of psychoanalysis . . . a venture in basic theorizing that is not to my taste" (p. 87).

KOHUT'S CRITIQUE OF THE IMPLICIT VALUE SYSTEM IN PSYCHOANALYSIS

Kohut felt that a shift in the basic analytic stance had occurred that he saw as more threatening than the by now recurring attempts by certain proponents of the medical profession to absorb and "streamline" psychoanalysis. From the point of view of intersubjectivity theory as described previously, it is interesting to note that Kohut (1984) objected to "an unacknowledged and unquestioned value system and . . . an unacknowledged and unquestioned total view of the essence of man and the essence of his life" (p. 89). He feared that psychoanalysis was becoming less of a science and more of a moral system, less of a scientific procedure and more of an educational procedure, with predetermined goals toward which the patient is led and which, "on the basis of an unacknowledged and unquestioned dimension of the transference, the patient tries to reach" (p. 89). He felt that these values had become predominant in psychoanalysis, leading analysts to selective perception, action, and goals instead of allowing patients to unfold and expand from the basis of what we would call their subjective worlds.

What are the values that are central to traditional psychoanalysis, and which are seen as the basis of the scientific objectivity of metapsychology, the very definition of science that Kohut criticized and to which he offered an alternative in his revolutionary papers on empathy? (1959, 1982) They are "independence" and "knowledge" values. Independence values see a man's or woman's "life from childhood to adulthood [as] a move forward from a position of helplessness, dependence and shameful clinging to a position of power, independence and proud autonomy," and "this assumption takes for granted that the undesirable features of adulthood, the flaws in the adult's psychic organization, must be conceptualized as manifestations of a psychological infantilism, that is, as manifestations of psychic immaturity due to the failure to move forward in development or due to a person's frightened return to the weakness, dependence and clinging attitudes of the child" (Kohut, 1980, p. 480). Kohut called this value system a "maturation morality" (p. 480). He believed that the predominance of independence values was based on the dominant position of knowledge values, which he saw as a part of drive theory. Here the goal is to see reality clearly despite unpleasure and to achieve the developmental step from the pleasure principle to the reality principle via the taming or sublimation of the drives. In this view, Freud saw humans both in "his individual development and in history as submitting only reluctantly to the domesticating influences of civilization and as falling woefully short of the moral-developmental ideal which demands that he tame his drives and assert his intelligence" (Kohut, 1980, pp. 480–481).

Kohut (1980) acknowledged that these values were in accordance with "the prevailing value system of Western Civilization" (p. 480). In fact, as a member of Western civilization, he felt deeply influenced by them and also pointed out how difficult it is to even become aware of them. The problem that this value system poses is twofold. The first problem is whether we are able to reflect in our clinical work on how our value system, our "prejudices," influence the intersubjective field and how they are deeply implicated in our patients' transferences. The problem here is not only the value system per se but also its claim to universality, to objectivity. In the preceding chapter, we began to spell out intersubjectivity theory's answer to this conundrum. The other problem is the abiding primacy allotted to these values in the hierarchy of human values. The alternative that Kohut offered in his theory of self psychology will be taken up later. For Kohut (1984), it "wasn't the isolated inconsistency of the intrusion of a vague and insipid biological concept into [Freud's] marvelous system of psychology that would have spurred [him] toward scientific action" (p. 91).

In fact, it was the work of two American ego psychologists greatly respected by Kohut, Franz Alexander and Heinz Hartmann, that triggered Kohut (1984) to "outline the operationally determined borders of psychoanalysis and thus to define the essence of this science" (p. 88). Specifically, he criticized Alexander's introduction of the psychosociological concept of "man's oral-drive-fueled inclination toward dependence" (pp. 87–88) and his psychobiological explanation of various medical syndromes "via the pivotal concept of the vector of 'the drives'" (p. 87) as well as Hartmann's psychosociological concept of "an adaptive point of view." However, Kohut's critique was aimed not at what he described as "valuable and impressive contributions to science" (p. 88) but rather at the introduction of these concepts as expansions of psychoanalysis rather than, as he saw it, as applications of psychoanalysis to the field of social psychology.

In other words, his criticism was aimed at the fact that these concepts were not identified as belonging to a different level of scientific discourse.

He saw them as "foreign bodies in depth psychology—the biologically understood concept of 'drive,' the sociopsychologically understood concepts of 'dependence' and 'adaptation,'" which led "to the decisive shift of the essence of analysis, to an alteration of the analyst's basic stance that is more significant in the long run than external threats" (Kohut, 1984a, pp. 88–89) to psychoanalysis. Interestingly, it is precisely at this point that European psychoanalysts have criticized American analysts for misrepresenting Freud. While there certainly is validity to the critique of a misleading translation of Freud (see Bettelheim, 1983), which, coupled with American pragmatism, led to a too mechanistic interpretation of Freud and an unacknowledged view of the purpose of psychoanalysis as too aligned with making patients able to function, this does not invalidate Kohut's critique of a hidden value system in traditional psychoanalysis leading to unacknowledged extraneous goals in psychoanalytic treatment, or, more to the point, the validity of Kohut's intention of defining psychoanalysis as pure psychology.

Kohut (1980) stresses that Freud, after he turned from neurophysiology and neurology to consistently using a psychological approach in his explorations and unambiguously speaking of psychoanalysis as psychology, was never able to completely give up his "thought habits of his first professional commitments" (p. 488). Instead, he developed "his theories within a syncretistic framework—put less kindly, we might speak of a misalliance—that has come to be known as psychobiology" (p. 488). He singles out the concept of the drive as part of Freud's metapsychology as a concept that "introduces all kinds of confusion and ambiguity" (p. 488) and that, for instance, if we are speaking of the mind as processing drives, is so disconcerting because "in the middle of the sentence we are suddenly pitchforked from one level of discourse to the other" (p. 489). It is not that we ignore sexuality or aggression—yes, there is desire and anger after experiencing cohesion; rather, we object to their decontextualization. Insofar as we regard meaning and the search for meaning as primary for human motivation, we ask how a particular person experiences sexuality or aggression in a particular context. Why is this significant? Are we suffering from scientific nitpicking in the service of pedantry or purism or, worse, simply to denigrate Freud's monumental achievement? I think not, and I will attempt to explain further why such a detailed discussion of empathy is indeed necessary.

PERSONAL MEANING VERSUS OBJECTIVE "TRUTH"

The point I am making is connected to the myth of objectivity and neutrality and the deleterious consequences for analytic listening and to our understanding of the relationship between mode of observation and theory. If we maintain a psychobiological stance, then we can make the claim of possessing the scientific, objective truth about our patients. In Schwaber's (1981) words, analytic listening has "continued to maintain a material reality alongside that of the patient's subjective view. . . . Analytic listening has employed the use of two realities—that of the observer from the outside, and that from within . . . the patient's subjective reality. Thus there are two realities—one internal, the other external; one that the patient experiences or perceives, the other that the analyst 'knows.' However we may choose to deal with this technically, analytic listening, embedded in this dual vantage point, must ultimately imply that the aim is to help the patient gradually shift or 'correct' his view as he attains more mature functioning" (p. 149). Thus, if we maintain a material reality alongside the subjective reality in form of, for instance, the biological concept of the drives, this lends itself to becoming unwittingly amalgamated to a stance that claims to possess the objective truth about the inner world of the patient. The unacknowledged shifting back and forth between material and subjective reality, between an extrospective and an introspective stance, hinders the process of contextualizing a psychological experience by claiming a universal truth that the analyst is privy to and the patient is not. This scientifically muddled flipping between two levels of discourse has major consequences for the understanding of patients, for the relationship between patient and analyst and between the mode of observation and theory, and, finally, for theory itself. For example, if we conceptualize the borderline states as being based on the aggressive drive, we may be stopped in our investigation of the context of a patient's aggression by simply claiming that the patient is a priori prone to destructiveness and a borderline disorder. In my experience, this leads some candidates and therapists to emphatically exclaim, "That's aggressive" or "He (or she) is a borderline" in regard to a patient's experience, as if nothing more needs to be said. In the worst case, patients are told that they *are* "borderline" and thus come to feel stigmatized and in danger of being deported beyond the realm of the human. While one could argue about the etiology of any given disorder, the more profound and subtle issue I am addressing is the effect on our clinical sensibility. There is also an implicit issue of power tucked away and well hidden from ourselves if we adhere to the dual vantage point. If directly asked, few therapists would be inclined to see themselves as not searching for the patient's truth, but the siren call of omniscience, masked as objectivity, has an appeal not to be underestimated.

This confusion of the levels of discourse led to the curious situation that of the two realities existing in any psychoanalytic situation—that of the patient and that of the analyst—the patient's reality was ultimately considered to be of secondary importance to the analyst's view of the patient's reality. It was George Klein who already in 1973 offered an explanation—very close to Kohut's later view—for this predicament in his paper "Two Theories or One?" Klein stated that psychoanalysis contains in actuality two kinds of theory, one clinical and one metapsychological, that essentially are incompatible. Metapsychology is a reflection of Freud's philosophy of science, which saw mentalistic concepts as temporary expedients that were to be ultimately reduced to the terms of physiological mechanisms. It was Klein's contention that metapsychology is not distinctly psychoanalytic in that "it reduces human behavior to a conceptual domain which requires a kind of observational datum different from that available in the psychoanalytic situation. . . . Metapsychology throws overboard the fundamental intent of the psychoanalytic enterprise—that of unlocking [personal] meanings. . . . Even if finer levels of physiological occurrences were measurable during the analytic hour, physiological theory would never be primary for the personal meanings of such events—their psychological significance require so-called mentalistic and teleological terms" (Klein, 1973, p. 109).

Just as unlocking personal meanings is fundamental for the psychoanalytic process, so is the subjectivity of the theorist, as noted previously, closely linked to his or her theory. Kohut (1984) mentions that ever since his childhood, he was familiar with the relativity of our perceptions of reality as well as the "relativity of the framework of ordering concepts that shape our observations and explanations" (p. 90). In his paper "Introspection, Empathy, and Psychoanalysis" (1959), he made clear what this basic stance means for the field of depth psychology: that reality, per se, whether extrospective or introspective, is unknowable and "*that we can only describe what we see within the framework of what we have done to see it*" (p. 91, emphasis added). In passing, Kohut mentions that this stance is analogous to developments in other sciences, in particular modern physics and the work of Einstein, Planck, and Heisenberg: here a new kind of objectivity is posited, "namely a scientific objectivity which includes the subjective" (p. 90).

For Kohut, the framework of observation is through introspection in ourselves and through empathy, which he defined as vicarious introspection, for others. Introspection and empathy are the framework of what we have done to see it. He differentiates between observations of physical phenomena that involve using our senses (extrospection) and observation of psychological phenomena "when the essential ingredient of our observation is introspection and empathy" (Kohut, 1959, p. 206). "Only a phenomena that we can attempt to observe by introspection or by empathy with another's introspection may be called psychological. A phenomena is 'somatic,' 'behavioristic,' or 'social' if our methods of observation do not predominantly include introspection and empathy" (pp. 208–209). Thus, if we use our sensory organs to observe the external world, our investigations will bring us observational data about physical phenomena. But how do we observe thoughts, wishes, and feelings, phenomena that cannot be touched, heard, or seen but that are nonetheless real? Why are introspection and empathy necessary to observe psychological as opposed to physical phenomena? Kohut gives a simple example: in observing an unusually tall person, this person's size will naturally influence our psychological assessment. "Without introspection and empathy, however, his size remains simply a physical attribute. Only when we think ourselves into his place, only when we, by vicarious introspection, begin to feel his unusual size as if it were our own and thus revive inner experiences in which we had been unusual or conspicuous, only then do we begin to appreciate the *meaning* that the unusual size may have for this person and only then have we observed a psychological fact" (pp. 207–208).

Why have self psychologists and intersubjectivists gone to such great lengths to explain the primacy of subjectivity as opposed to the role of reality, truth, and objectivity in understanding the therapeutic process? For Kohut, as I hope I have been able to make clear, the experience-distant values of knowledge and independence and the biological concept of the drive reflect belief systems that are portrayed as universal, objective truths applicable to all human beings. As such, they hinder the understanding of the personal meanings that each of these concepts may have for the individual patient. This, in turn, may block our ability to understand a patient's subjective experience and the role we have in the occurrence of a particular experience at a particular time. In other words, it wouldn't take the intersubjective field into account in which a highly individual self-experience arises or recedes.

CLINICAL VIGNETTES

Two clinical vignettes will be helpful to illustrate what is meant by the primacy of subjectivity, the role of the empathic-introspective listening stance, and the intersubjective field. A patient reports that she feels "like a lump, like nothing." I feel uncomfortable with her experience and make a defensive interpretation. I say, "Perhaps you have some feelings about me that you shy away from." "No," she responded, "I feel like a blank screen." This was a patient who suffered from depressive feelings of emptiness, despair, and hopelessness. At the time, I was defensively warding off resonating introspectively with what felt like a psychic black hole to me, evoking a fear of being pulled into infinite nothingness. Therefore, I pushed the patient further with another attempt to explain her experience as a particular kind of reaction to me. In exasperation, she cried out, "There's nothing behind that screen, it's blank." Clearly, in making an interpretation that she was experiencing anxiety about feelings toward me as a separate person, I had committed a technical error that reflected more of my own selfobject needs to be seen—albeit as the target of repressed and anxious feelings (as well as my need to ward off my own painful reaction)—than the self-state of the patient. The session ended in a disturbed, diffuse atmosphere. The next session, she came in reporting triumphantly that she'd had a dream in which she had shot me. This time I was able to understand that in the previous session, she had experienced me as a threat to her vulnerable sense of self and had responded by mobilizing a cohesion-repairing feeling of aggression.

The vignette is a good illustration of why Kohut called empathy a plodding, data-gathering process, as well as the analyst's inability to sustain a method of inquiry, guided by a trial-and-error search for meaning. It also shows how I was unable to tolerate avoiding closure due to a block in my ability to be introspective and exemplifies the concept of mutual regulation in the intersubjective field. I will return to the difficulties for the therapist encountered in the process of introspection.

In a case reported by a supervisee, a patient decribed a scene from childhood: during the building of a house, her parents had taken her along to the building site and, to avoid the possibility of injury, had tied her to a chair for many hours. The patient, who had been physically abused by both parents over many years, spoke of this experience in glowing terms: finally, her parents had had a joint venture that kept them from fighting and in which the patient was allowed to participate and finally have a deeper feeling of being at home, of having arrived. At the time, the patient and her analyst were trying to understand why the patient lived in a building that was supposed to be renovated but that seemed to be a dangerous place to live because the patient was the only tenant left and because, other than the scaffolding's having been erected, nothing further had been done in quite some time, thus making her potentially an easy target for criminals. The patient's adult relationships were characterized by abuse. The analyst attempted to connect the patient's felt necessity to sacrifice herself in a masochistic mode in order to benefit from or maintain a tie. Although her interpretation was undoubtedly correct in regard to a central organizing principle of her patient, in the hierarchy of motivations that were salient in this particular session, the analyst missed the experience of the patient. The patient felt vitalized in her memory of belonging and strengthened by her ability to lock out danger and maintain a sense of safety within her own apartment. The building site she lived on reminded her of one of the few instances of feeling at home in her past. This does not mean that the analyst was incorrect in dealing with the larger issues of safety and less harmful prerequisites of maintaining ties. Nonetheless, as we shall come to see, the building blocks of felt cohesion are small indeed. The sequence of understanding is paramount for the development of a sense of self. In this case, the patient would have first needed an acknowledgment of her vitalized feeling within the framework that she was able to experience it and not how the therapist experienced it. One can speculate whether it might have been the analyst's own introspectively felt sense of endangerment that led to the analyst's being unable to tolerate the patient's experience, which would have enabled her to wait with her interpretation concerning the patient's felt need to undergo threat as a prerequisite to receiving attention.

ANALYTIC "TRUTH": AN EMERGENT CHARACTERISTIC OF DIALOGUE

Kohut defined empathy as vicarious introspection, as the ability to grasp the inner life of another human being by going into resonance with the feeling states of the other. This is not as easy as it may seem because we may only *think* we are in resonance with the other person and, as we could see in the clinical examples, jump to incorrect conclusions. Schematically, we could describe the listening process in the following way: we listen to what a patient tells us, we go into inner resonance with his or her experience looking for similar experiences in ourselves, then we go back to the patient's experience and check whether we mean approximately the same thing. As a result of our dialogue, we arrive at an approximation of the patient's experience—an approximation because we can, as analytic listeners, never abandon our own frame of reference. We can only view our patient's subjectivity through the lens of our own subjectivity and see whether we can agree on a truth that is as close as possible to the patient's view. This is why Orange et al. (1997) speak of analytic "truth" as *emerging* as a result of a dialogue. The "truth" is in fact found at the intersection of the two subjectivities involved, but it is the process of empathy that provides the basis for us—in connection with dialogue—to arrive at an approximation of the patient's experience.

Stolorow and his colleagues conceptualized the empathic *process* as a process of empathic-introspective *inquiry*. Inquiry denotes what Kohut meant with the data-gathering, plodding, trial-and-error process, which demands a forbearance of quick closure in order to attempt to view the patient from within his or her framework. Along similar lines, Orange (1995) has asked us to wear our theoretical coats lightly, being willing to shed them easily if we see that they are an obstacle to understanding. No one means quite the same thing with any given word or feeling, as whole worlds of subjective experience shape the personal meanings of the words that we use. Empathy is so difficult because it demands a constant self-questioning and self-reflective stance. In a sense, we have to constantly and simultaneously plummet into our self-experience and question it in terms of its relevance for the patient. This requires a lengthy training that, as arduous as it never ceases to be, can at the same time become what I would call an acquired taste. Over the years, as my listening skills have been honed, I have found that it can be a thrill to try to capture the initially alien-seeming nuance of the other's experience, in a certain regard, precisely because it is so foreign to me. The development and maintenance of our sense of curiosity—a stance of not knowing but of perpetually searching for an understanding of personal meanings—is what makes our work exciting and keeps us from deadening feelings of repetition. Learning to be empathic is a difficult task, a skill that takes some length of time to acquire, that can never be fully accomplished, and that requires an ongoing discipline. Every therapist tries to understand his or her patient: I have often heard this as being a somewhat banal given and therefore as a critique of empathy. Of course, this is true, but not every therapist tries to understand the patient as the patient understands him- or herself, and not every therapist understands the worlds of difference in perspective and how treacherously easy it is for us all to assume that we understand. More will be said to explain the complexity of understanding from the intersubjective viewpoint later in this chapter.

An interim summary: Introspection, here defined as going into resonance with the other by reflecting on our own analogous experiences, including specifically our own unconscious organizing principles that determine our frame of reference, is the baseline of empathic inquiry. Empathy is the *process* through which we attempt approximation of the patient's view, including an understanding of his or her unconscious organizing principles. Empathy is the process of checking that there is a relative match between our resonance to the patient and how the patient sees him- or herself. The "match" is actually a dialogically developed "truth" that emerges out of the intersection of the two subjectivities. As is readily discernible, this is one of the reasons we speak of the analyst–patient dyad as an indissoluble unit.

PROBLEMS OF INTROSPECTION

Returning to the difficulties for the therapist in the process of introspection, Kohut (1959) was still pouring new wine into old bottles so that he initially described the resistance to introspection in energic terms: thought, or introspection, seems to oppose the relief from tension found through action and leads to the unpleasurable damming of energy. The inability to release energy leads a person to experience introspection as a form of helplessness and passivity that can express itself as an itchy restlessness. In terms of contemporary affect theory, we might reconceptualize the unpleasurable damming of energy as the inability to contain expansive or painful affect states due to a lack of soothing experiences in the past that would have helped integrate overwhelming affects and not allow them to spiral into painful states. Later, Kohut was able to contextualize the intrapsychic experience of introspection by conceptualizing the resistance in terms of a fear that our meanings will differ from others' and thereby we will run the risk of severing the self-sustaining bond to our empathic environment. Prolonged breaches in this bond—sustained separations from the responsive understanding of others—lead to the deepest separation anxiety, namely, the annihilation of self-experience. This fear will be evoked not only by an actual loss of self-sustaining persons but also by the process of introspection itself, which can lead to a shift in the perception of the self-sustaining selfobject imago, and then be experienced as equally threatening to a person's sense of a cohesive self-experience. Going back to our first clinical vignette, I might have gone into resonance with the patient's felt lack of vitality, which in turn may have evoked similar experiences of a lack of a responsive experiential world, eliciting my defensive reaction against painful feelings of an inner void—empty inner halls echoing out of my past. Mutual regulation, I must again emphasize, is a concept that one can perhaps readily grasp, but living and working with it is an entirely different matter: the walls of our monadic castles, as stated before, are very attractive for our sense of security. In regard to the selfobject needs of therapists, had I been as schooled in intersubjectivity theory then, some 20 years ago, as I am now, I might have been able to better reflect on my unconscious need for self-sustaining contact with the patient and would have been able to decenter more rapidly from this need, having reflected on it as a possibly normal occurrence in an intersubjective field and therefore not having to repress such a reflection into the netherworld of neutrality.

This alludes to another hindrance to introspection, namely, that the concept of mutual regulation entails taking responsibility for the effect that our perceptual frame of reference may have on patients. Again, a clinical example from a supervisee: his patient spoke with enthusiasm about a fellow student in her high school psychology class who spoke very openly about her suicidal thoughts. The supervisee went into resonance with the student's exposure of intimate life details in a relatively unprotected environment and therefore asked his patient whether she didn't identify with the student's vulnerable self-exposure. In the back of his mind was the patient's difficulty in opening up areas of vulnerability in treatment and his own unreflected need to be protective of her. With his intervention, however, he stressed the danger because he felt outraged at the lack of protection offered by the teacher. The patient was stressing a different point: she identified with the freedom of expression on the part of her fellow student, not with a sense of threat. In our discussion, we were able to see and productively discuss how difficult it can be to loosen the hold of our own deeply felt convictions, as well intended as they may be, and to return to the track of the patient's experience, as well as understand how we obstruct the further unfolding of the patient's subjective world by sticking to what seems to us to make the most common sense. Thus, while it may seem quite reasonable to challenge the patient's perception, subjectively we can be miles apart from his or her reality.

This example may be useful to further clarify Kohut's scientific definition of empathy, to differentiate it from its usage in common language, and to preclude viewing empathy as "an outgrowth of vague sentimentality or mysticism" (Kohut, 1984b, p. 85). To reiterate, Kohut conceptualized empathy as an information-gathering, data-collecting activity, or process. He did not write about empathy as associated with any specific emotion, such as compassion or affection. In fact, he pointed out that empathy can be motivated and used for hostile-destructive aims; it takes knowledge of an enemy to attack his weak spots. Empathy is for the most part used nonintuitively, ploddingly, by trial and error; as such it is neither always correct nor always accurate. It is seen as a precondition for being supportive and therapeutic, but, used in this sense, it is not supportive or therapeutic by itself. As an instrument of observation, it functions as an *informer* of therapeutic and psychoanalytic action.

We distinguish this understanding of empathy from the popular usage when we speak of an empathic person, as in this definition we assume that it usually leads to correct results. It was such an experience-distant concept of empathy that could lead the therapist to think that his patient was in need of protection. If we use the term *empathy* in a depth-psychological sense as an attempt to understand the inner life of another person, then we would have felt impelled to take the plodding, trial-and-error route to ascertain what the experience in fact did mean for this particular patient and try to understand her as she understood herself. In this sense, patients are our teachers, and we are perpetual students of their inner worlds. In popular usage, empathy signifies being nice to someone on the grounds of felt compassion. In psychoanalysis, empathy means *understanding*—nothing more and nothing less. To understand the patient in his or her terms is what is meant by the primacy of subjectivity. Interestingly, this task often is not viewed as the fundamental task of psychotherapy but instead has become the rationale for gross misunderstandings of the centrality of the empathic-introspective stance of inquiry in self psychology as well as in intersubjectivity theory and practice. In its most extreme forms, empathy has been criticized as naive, as a view of the world seen through rosy Disneyland lenses. Strangely, understanding the patient seems then to become confused with coddling patients by blending out the harsher realities of life.

Given that this confusion (not to say gross misunderstanding of empathy) is still prevalent to this day, it is understandable why Kohut was hesitant to seemingly contradict everything he had said about empathy as an information-gathering activity that simply *informs* therapeutic action and to add that empathy per se also has a beneficial therapeutic effect. He feared "abandoning scientific sobriety and . . . entering the land of mysticism and sentimentality" (Kohut, 1984b, p. 85). It was, however, also his scientific hypothesis "that the fear of death and the fear of psychosis are . . . the expression of the fear of the loss of the empathic milieu that in responding to the self keeps it *psychologically* alive" (p. 86). In his view, humans are dependent on empathic responsiveness from the cradle to the grave. Clearly, this corresponds to the intersubjective view of the unbearable embeddedness of being. The denial of dependence, or the intersubjective foundation of all living beings, is the very source of the critique of empathy as an immature sentimental stance, indulging the other, a critique that, one could be tempted to hypothesize, ironically may have its developmental origins in the very lack of experience of an empathic milieu.

THE CLINICAL EFFECT OF THE EMPATHIC-INTROSPECTIVE STANCE

Let me now, as promised at the beginning of this chapter and in response to the "sentimentality" critique, turn to the *clinical* application and the *clinical effect* of the empathic-introspective stance in treatment because, as we shall see, "empathy, the understanding of the patient's subjective reality, *does* have direct clinical consequences. For many of our patients the basic reason for their suffering, or even for a lack of a (positive) cohesive sense of self in space and over time, lies in the fact that they either do not know, trust, or are in conflict about their own perceptions (and their concommitant affective states). Empathy, or the close adherence to the patient's view of the world, therefore serves a fundamental curative purpose in that the patient's experience of the uniqueness of his or her perspective of reality is no longer felt as a threat to themselves or others" (Jaenicke, 1993, p. 257). "For many patients it is a novel experience to have their viewpoints consistently and reliably understood. It introduces them to the possibility of reliability and consistency in their perceptions of themselves and the other" (p. 258) and, in time, to a more reliable sense of selfhood and an increased ability to believe in and make use of the emotional availability of the other. "In comparison to the patient's past experience this effect of empathy is in fact a corrective emotional experience. A sharp distinction must be made, however, between the patient's experience of empathy and a directive, manipulative approach on the part of the analyst" (p. 258). I will return to this point later, especially in chapter three. Let us focus now on the effect of empathy on the patient's sense of self. "The reflection of the *manifest* content of the patient's productions allows the patient to *identify*, in many instances for the first time, with what he or she is feeling and thinking" (p. 258). In terms of the latent, or unconscious, content, we can begin our search for understanding the unconscious organizing principles from which these thoughts and feelings have emerged and which have coalesced into unreflected belief systems. Therefore, a further function of empathy is "that it provides a medium through which such belief systems can become crystallized, brought into awareness, and examined" (p. 258).

Two points need to be stressed here, points that, perhaps because they are so directly in front of our analytic noses and therefore may also seem not complex enough for analytic minds trained to understand the labyrinths of the unconscious and accustomed to thinking around three corners, are often overlooked. The seemingly simple task of reflecting the patient back to him- or herself on a manifest content level is not simply a parroting of the obvious or a timid paraphrasing to coddle the patient into believing the world is a warm bath of understanding that he or she unfortunately missed in the cruel world of their childhood. In fact, it is returning to the patient lost bits of self-experience that through the medium of empathy, or affect attunement, allows him or her to feel and integrate what they have said and thus to achieve a more profound and reflective sense of self. Often, only through the feedback loop of reflection does the patient connect what he or she has said to themselves. Without our resonance, patients may experience the hour as a rush of words and leave the session feeling frazzled, confused, and unbound. This is also, of course, in accordance with infant research, such as Stern's (1985) view that the birth, maintenance, and transformation of the sense of self and other occurs in an intersubjective context. The first point, therefore, is that empathy, or understanding the manifest level of the patient's productions, has a *cohesive function* for the patient. This is a point that lends itself to being overlooked by analysts trained in the drive-defense model because this analytic listening stance may direct the analyst to undervalue or disregard the function of understanding the manifest level in favor of a bias for hidden meanings, thus unwittingly further destabilizing the patient's view of him- or herself. Rather than consolidating an unstable sense of self, the patient may experience a fragmentation of him- or herself as he or she is offered yet another view of him- or herself, much like the multiple reflections seen in a hall of mirrors. The second point I wish to stress is that, for most people, it is a new experience *to have someone attempt to understand them as they understand themselves*. Friends are more likely to advise, to tell their own stories of similar experiences, or to avoid holding the self-state of the person they are listening to because it is felt as a threat to their own sense of self, and they therefore feel impelled to offer a solution, to solve the problem, and thus to distance themselves from understanding. Originally, it was the faulty affect attunement of the main caregivers that makes the understanding of the patient on what Kohut called the low road of empathy, the experience-near mode of listening so significant for comprehending the clinical effect of understanding.

Understanding a patient on the manifest level is not a linear process; however, the necessity to do so will be determined by the extent of vulnerability and fragility of self-experience in combination with the extent of the faulty attunement in the past. "No perception of self-experience will be questioned as long as it serves a vital cohesion-maintaining function" (Jaenicke, 1993, p. 259). The issue for the patient who lacks a cohesive self-experience is to preserve the status quo of selfhood, "however precariously established and stifled in its functions it may be" (Kohut, 1984b, p. 114). Actually, this short Kohut quote not only applies to patients lacking cohesion but also contains the key to understanding the clinical function of empathy as well as understanding a fundamental aspect of the self-psychological and intersubjective stance in treatment in regard to all patients. The issue here is the central role that *safety* has for patients. Only if clinicians are aware of this most basic need will they be able to empathically interpret the patient's productions that on the surface may seem self-destructive or aggressive and where our first reaction may be, How can they do that to themselves or us? In this context, I would like to paraphrase the famous quote by Bill Clinton, whose first presidential campaign was successful because he understood the phrase devised by his campaign chief, "It's not the war; it's the economy, stupid!" Analogously, for many patients we need to tell ourselves, "It's not aggression; it's fear, stupid." I will only touch on two related issues at this point: the issue of conflict and the issue of defense resistances. "It is only when patients have been allowed to achieve a basic trust in their perceptions, feelings, thoughts that they can begin to experience those aspects of themselves that are unknown or contradictory" (Jaenicke, 1993, p. 258) and that are therefore experienced as threatening and dangerous. "It is at this point [of felt safety] that they will spontaneously manifest the less logical, less rational, random, hitherto unacceptable aspects of themselves. In other words, while the unconscious certainly codetermined the patient's material all along, it is only now that the patient will feel safe enough to acknowledge and integrate it. It is only from this vantage point that conflict will begin to play an increasingly important role, because the ability to tolerate conflict presupposes a minimum of self-cohesion" (p. 259). In their book *Psychoanalysis of Developmental Arrests*, Stolorow and Lachmann (1980) describe the figure–ground relationship between the experience of safety within the selfobject tie and the ability to experience conflict. Defense-resistances need to be understood—as Kohut pointed out in 1984—in terms of the psychic organization as a whole, rather than as discrete, delimited mechanisms of a mental apparatus. If they are understood as *defensive structures* laid down to perform certain self-preserving functions, then defense-analysis will deal with understanding and exploring the subjective dangers the patient experiences in the analytic relationship. "The purpose of empathy is to amplify such feeling-states to the point where they are no longer a part of a pre-reflective (that is, unconscious) organizing principle. Only after (such) self-states have been acknowledged, validated and integrated will the possibility of experiencing conflict become relevant. Once they are acknowledged as a valid aspect of selfhood, an ensuing conflict with another equally valid central striving need not be experienced as annihilating (or threatening) to the integrity of self-experience" (Jaenicke, 1993, p. 259). In intersubjectivity theory, both conflict and defense resistances are seen not only as intrapsychic phenomena; instead, the intrapsychic has been contextualized so that conflict and defense resistances are seen to have their origins in intersubjective fields of the past and are seen to arise and recede in treatment in accordance with how the patient experiences the intersubjective field created by the patient–therapist dyad as well as the intersubjective worlds they are embedded in.

MISUNDERSTANDINGS ABOUT EMPATHY

Returning to the concept of empathy, we need to explore further why empathy has been misunderstood as sympathy and at the same time address the issue of why some analysts have given self psychology the seemingly condemning attribute of being supportive psychotherapy rather than psychoanalysis proper. In this view, self psychology is seen as a helpful adjunct to traditional psychoanalysis, which is, however, reserved for a certain subcategory of patients, namely, the narcissistic personality disorders. The implication here is that self psychology and the empathic stance are relevant for the more fragile, pre-oedipally disturbed patients, while "real" analysis deals with the central human issues of sexuality and aggression. Intersubjectivists do not see narcissistic issues as a distinct diagnostic criteria but rather view narcissism as a *dimen-*

sion of self-experience and of every transference relevant for all patients. Kohut (1980, 1982) was the first to point out the maturational morality implicit in Freud's view of narcissism as becoming transformed into the more mature form of object love. This is where things get muddy and psychoanalytic concepts slide into one another like too many layers of paint: self psychology and the empathic-introspective stance are seen as a supportive method to deal with a very fragile patient population that necessitates a sympathetic stance on the part of the therapist. I can hear the outcry of many colleagues who would disagree with this description as polemical. Nonetheless, as I am speaking about a continuum of basic analytic attitudes, beginning at one end with a differentiated discussion of analytic concepts and ending at the other end with more diffuse deeply held beliefs coalescing into difficult-to-pinpoint analytic attitudes toward patients, I must uphold the necessity for a detailed discussion of what empathy is and what it is not. I wish it were not necessary to restate issues that Kohut began writing about over 40 years ago, but empathy plays a central role in the development of psychoanalysis as well as for intersubjectivity theory.

"If empathy were sympathy, rather than an attempt to understand patients as accurately as possible according to their own subjectivity, then the analyst would serve an approving or disapproving function. If this were the case, then analysis would be nothing more than an education in the analyst's subjective morality, rather than the revolutionary vehicle that Freud first envisioned. If that criticism were true, then self psychology would indeed fit Alexander's view of analysis as manipulating corrective emotional experiences. It is ironic that Kohut's (1959, 1982) concept of empathy, which emphasizes the uniqueness of the individual and thereby follows in Freud's footsteps in his upheaval of cultural norms, is misunderstood as a directive technique" (Jaenicke, 1993, p. 260).

The question now arises, Why *has* empathy been mistaken for sympathy? This is a crucial issue because the implicit subtext that colors discussions of self psychology is still overshadowed by the stigma of supportive psychotherapy versus analysis proper. "Underlying this view is the implicit assumption that the conscious content, the manifest productions of the patient, are not to be viewed as having the same value, as giving the same clinical yield as the unconscious, latent content. Here we have an important difference in the *clinical approach* to the unconscious. Self psychology has come under attack because the clinical *function* of empathy has been misunderstood. While the prolonged empathic understanding of the patient's *current* condition *seemingly* disregards the unconscious motivations, in actuality it *promotes* the emergence of thwarted developmental needs, archaic states, and the archaic bond" (Jaenicke, 1993, p. 260). It also provides an intersubjective context in which all disavowed or repressed affects or needs—no matter where they find their place on the continuum of the narcissistic dimension of the transference or whether they are expressions of conflictual material—can safely reemerge. "The consistent verbalizations of the patient's present inner states promotes archaic states and the archaic bond because it allows an imagined identity of inner experiences between the patient and the analyst to develop" (p. 261). "Examples of such states include the restoration of symbiotic-like merger which had been precipitously or phase-appropriately disrupted . . . [and] the reliance upon archaic selfobject configurations to sustain a vulnerable self representation" (Stolorow and Lachmann, 1980, pp. 175–176). The hitherto fragile and tentative self-feelings or affects can reemerge, expand, and fuse in fantasy with the analyst's imagined perfect selfhood. The analyst thus experienced by the patient as a source of infallible strength provides the patient with a cocoon in which the further unfolding and exploration of self-experience can take place (Jaenicke, 1993).

THE ISSUE OF RECEIVING PRESENTS AND ANSWERING QUESTIONS

The merger with the fantasized strength of the analyst allows a holding environment (Winnicott, 1965) to develop that gives the patient the safety to express affects that were previously connected to some sense of subjective danger. For instance, a patient of mine who had not been able to express her love and admiration for her father allowed such feelings to reemerge and expressed them in a concretized form by bringing me flowers. In this case, it behooved me to accept this expression of an idealizing selfobject transference with a simple thank-you rather than at this point in the psychotherapeutic treatment to offer an interpretation concerning the underlying unconscious motivation. This would only lead to a break in the bond with a renewed repression of the patient's expansive expression of a developmental need that was arrested by a similar lack of responsiveness in her childhood. The question whether this expression also serves a defensive function, such as undoing feelings of aggression toward the analyst or reestablishing an old mode of relatedness based on a belief that attention or interest of the other can be attained only at the price of some form of payment or self-abasement, could be salient at a later date, most likely at a time when the soothing function of idealization has led to an integration of expansive and exciting affects hitherto experienced as threatening to the self-experience of the patient or to the other. I did, however, ask the patient how it felt to bring flowers, and she answered with an image of a little girl running expectantly toward her father and wrapping her arms around his legs. Sometimes it is difficult to accept these expressions of idealization, as they can mobilize feelings of expansiveness in the analyst that he or she may find hard to integrate, as they may touch on painful affects of disavowed needs to be admired or to feel self-worth.

If we understand the traditional analytic rule of not accepting presents from our patients out of a fear of gratifying a derivative of a libidinal need and thus thwarting the chance for this need to become symbolized and thus transformed, then we are working within the drive-defense model, which does not include the psychological understanding of developmental needs that become reinstated in the form of the selfobject transferences. Why do we not see the silent acceptance, even in the concretized form of this clinical example, as acting out and thus as inimical to the psychoanalytic enterprise? The answer has partially been given in the explanation of the affect-integrative function of the idealizing transference. A further answer pertains to our empathic understanding of where the patient is on the continuum of developmental needs. In this case, my understanding of the patient was based on her early developmental need, which allowed her to express feelings of admiration in a developmentally concretistic, as opposed to a symbolic, manner. Therefore, my response took the form of what I have conceptualized as *concretistic empathy*, or *enacted empathy* (Jaenicke, 2001, p. 312). My response was not based on an absence of analytic, interpretative understanding, such as is meant by the term *acting out*. It was my *analytic*, or empathic, understanding of the meaning of the patient's gesture that led me to keep my interpretation to myself. It goes without saying that with a different patient, where the issue may indeed be a disavowal of angry feelings, an interpretation addressing this issue right away would be appropriate. Here we are dealing with a form of idealization, such as described by Kernberg (1975), where aggression plays a central part in the organizing principle of the patient and where idealization clearly has the defensive function of warding off aggressive affect.

Of course, a central goal of analysis informed by intersubjectivity theory, much like classical analysis, is to expand the reflective awareness of the patient's unconscious organizing principles. (The unconscious organizing principles are the building blocks of the personality. They are based on the unconscious emotional conclusions that we have drawn from the repeated interactions with our main caregivers. They are the "central themes, or emotional convictions that characterize a person's experiential world" [Stolorow, Atwood, and Orange, 2002, p. 117.) Nonetheless, our interventions must be guided by our empathic understanding of a patient at a particular moment in the therapeutic process. Most presents are not on the scale of a house, a boat, or a horse. Usually, the material worth is more in the range of a CD or something patients make themselves, such as one unique gift I received at the end of an analysis: a tissue box in the shape of a couch. Generally, my experience has been—although like everything that occurs in psychotherapy, it is not a good idea to make a universal technical rule out of any particular intervention—that, more often than not, it is helpful to accept presents unless our empathy leads us to the opposite reaction. Not infrequently, a present may encapsulate a move toward us, a new developmental step, a widening of the selfobject bond, allowing patients to affectively expand, to try out new feelings that were unacceptable in their past. Then it would be simply an error in humanity (Stone, 1961) or simply rude to turn them down, much like refusing to offer congratulations when patients mention their birthdays. Sometimes the point is that patients want to be able to do something for us. This can, as usual, have any number of meanings. Perhaps it is a signal that a shift in the transference has occurred, such as a move out of a symbiotic-like merger, where the patient is feeling more separate, more equal to us. Or, conversely, it can signal a strengthening of the idealizing selfobject tie. It cannot be overemphasized that in order for the patient to have the courage to feel deep feelings of affection for us, denoting a significant expansion of their ability to experience self-worth and to recognize the value of the other, he or she must be able to count on our ability and our courage to wholeheartedly accept such feelings. In terms of the risk of relatedness, this is not necessarily so easy, as it again pertains to our willingness to be touched, to widen ourselves and let the patient in, to make room for the patient in our affective "households." Even if the primary motivation is defensive, it will still most likely be amalgamated with some feeling of closeness to us. What should stop us from analyzing both aspects or just the defensive aspect? Our choice of intervention will be determined by our understanding of the pertinence of the leading edge or the trailing edge of the patient's transference. Are we dealing primarily with a developmentally new step, or are we dealing with the fear of retraumatization, or is it salient to address a state of ambivalence? Turning the patient down completely for the sake of an analytic ideal of abstinence entails the risk of the patient closing like an oyster, in which case both motivations, the defensive and the expansive meanings, may get lost. Purposely frustrating the patient, as we said earlier, can hardly be viewed as neutral, as it reflects a deeply held belief system of the therapist, including basic assumptions about human nature; likewise, from the patient's perspective, the purposeful frustration of his or her needs and wishes will hardly be experienced as neutral (Orange et al., 1997).

Another clinical example: An experienced colleague who had completed an analysis some time ago but felt the need for more treatment gives me a CD. I thank him without further comment. I know that the issue is reflected in a particular song that we had already discussed. I understand his present as a gesture of trust and affection. Silently, I make the interpretation that this is primarily a revival of an arrested idealizing selfobject transference toward the often absent father, even if on a manifest level the content of the song dealt with a mother awaiting and welcoming the return of her son. The next session, the patient thanks me for not interpreting his present. As Kohut pointed out repeatedly, it is often best not to initially interpret these transferences but rather to let them unfold. In this case, I was led by my understanding of the patient's need to express strong emotions in a moderate form, as it allowed him to express affection without a loss of his sense of integrity. To interpret at this point would have been counterproductive. It would have accentuated the asymmetry that the patient was able to silently allow and use as a source of strength without experiencing a loss of self-worth. With the patient who gave me flowers, we were able to verbalize the symbolic meaning at a later time, when such a verbalization didn't threaten the analytic bond. Whether we interpret a present depends on our understanding of its meaning. The same principle applies to the answering of questions. This approach to patients' presents and their questions could be criticized as reflecting my own theoretical bias. While this is quite true, it also serves well to illustrate the intersubjective view that all forms of treatment reflect the subjectivity of the clinician—including his or her theories. The issue is, once again, to be aware of how our subjectivity is implicated in treatment and that whatever choices we make with our interventions, they must be reflected in terms of how they affect the patient.

Returning now to the clinical function of empathy: "Self psychology views the manifest productions of the patient as existing somewhere along a continuum from archaically rooted, unconscious self-states to conscious, differentiated, and integrated self-states. The function of empathy is to serve as a medium by which partially formed, or repressed, or disavowed self-states can safely undergo the transition from a pre-reflective experience to becoming a more reflected experience on the continuum of a person' s subjectivity. Self psychology (and intersubjectivity theory) have reconceptualized the clinical value of dealing with the manifest level of the patient's productions by demonstrating how invariant, unconscious structures will change . . . via the medium of empathy, which includes the understanding and interpretation of defense-resistances, into increasingly flexible, articulated, conscious structures of subjectivity" (Jaenicke, 1993, p. 261).

In this chapter on the empathic-introspective mode of inquiry, I have examined at length Kohut's invaluable contribution "in the development of a post-Cartesian, fully contextual psychoanalytic psychology that recognizes the constitutive role of relatedness in the making of all experience" (Stolorow, Atwood, and Orange, 1999, p. 381). We have seen that beginning with his 1959 paper on empathy, Kohut was able to redefine the domain of psychoanalytic inquiry and theory. By arguing that a scientific theory has to be consistent with a scientific method of investigation, Kohut demonstrated that "the psychoanalytic method always included introspection and empathy as its central constituents, [and] only that which was in principle accessible to introspection and empathy belonged within the domain of psychoanalytic theory" (p. 382). In doing so, Kohut redefined psychoanalysis as a depth psychology of personal experience because only personal experience and its vicissitudes are accessible to the psychoanalytic method of investigation.

SIMILARITIES AND DIFFERENCES BETWEEN SELF PSYCHOLOGY AND INTERSUBJECTIVITY THEORY

Because this is a book about intersubjectivity theory in practice and about the risks of relatedness in particular—an attempt to shed light on the contextuality of the psychoanalytic experience for both the patient and the therapist—and not self psychology, it is now necessary to discuss some of the fundamental similarities and differences between Kohut's view and intersubjectivity theory. This, in turn, will enable us to discuss similarities and differences between Kohut's concept of empathy and the intersubjective concept of empathic-introspective inquiry. It is a common misunderstanding that intersubjectivity theory was an outgrowth or extension of self psychology. In fact, the two theories were developed separately, originating from different points but coming to a similar conclusion, redefining psychoanalysis as pure psychology. Intersubjectivity theory, as was pointed out earlier, had its beginnings in the study of the subjective origins of theoretical systems in psychoanalysis. Having understood that the subjective world of a theorist profoundly influences his or her understanding of other persons' experiences, Stolorow and Atwood (1979) came to the conclusion that what psychoanalysis needed was a theory of subjectivity itself: "a unifying framework that could account not only for the phenomena that other theories address but also for the theories themselves" (Stolorow , Atwood and Orange, 1999, p. 381). In their view, psychoanalytic theory was to be—at all levels of abstraction and generality—"a depth psychology of personal experience, concerned with its development, its unconscious organization, and its therapeutic transformation" (p. 381). The subjective origins of psychoanalytic theories led the intersubjectivists to the centrality of phenomenology, which in turn led to the recognition of the primacy of a thoroughly contextualized subjectivity. "Subjectivity, we came to realize, can only be the experience of a historically situated subject. To be an experiencing subject is to be positioned in the intersubjective contexts of past, present, and future. Husserl's phenomenological reduction is transformed into a phenomenological elaboration of complexity and process, as properties of larger relational systems. Unremitting focus on the organization of personal experience, eschewing all isolated, reified mental entities, unveils the inescapable embeddedness of personal experience in constitutive intersubjective fields. Freud's ([1923] 1961) intrapsychic determinism gives way to a thoroughgoing intersubjective contextualism" (Stolorow, Atwood, and Orange, 1999, p. 382). Unbeknownst to the intersubjectivists, Kohut (1959) had arrived at this progression from phenomenology to contextualism through his examination of empathy. Another similarity between Kohut's self psychology and intersubjectivity theory that also exemplifies the move to a contextualist theory of psychoanalysis was his replacement of the concept of the drive with the subjective experience of drivenness, which is an affect state. This is of paramount theoretical importance, as it heralds the paradigmatic shift in psychoanalysis from a drive to an affect theory. This shift is a hallmark of intersubjectivity theory "because, unlike drives, which originate deep within the interior of an isolated mental apparatus, affectivity is something that from birth onward is regulated, or misregulated, within an ongoing intersubjective system. Thus the shift from drive to affect automatically entails a contextualization of human motivation" (Stolorow, Atwood, and Orange, 1999, p. 382).

Stolorow and Atwood were originally academic psychologists who hoped that their psychoanalytic phenomenology could provide a unifying framework for the fragmented field of comparative personality theory and thus recover the importance of studying the experience and conduct of persons in academic personality psychology. Kohut, in contrast, was not an academician but a psychoanalytic clinician (Jaenicke, 1999; Stolorow et al., 1999). Known in his time as Mr. Psychoanalysis, at one point vice president of the International Psychoanalytic Association, Kohut was originally a prominent proponent and gifted teacher of classical psychoanalysis. In the mid-1960s, he was led by the clinical experience that his patients did not seem to fit into or respond to his classical psychoanalytic understanding of their experiences to focus on the narcissistic dimension of their problems. Thus, his phenomenological understanding of his patients led to a variant of contextualism that opened up the path to an understanding—hitherto thwarted by Cartesian thought—of experiences of personal annihilation (Orange et al., 1997) that greatly influenced the intersubjectivists. The concept of the selfobject function (Kohut, 1971), already implicit in Kohut's 1959 paper on empathy, became a central concept for self psychology. By demonstrating how the organization of self-experience is always codetermined by the experience of the felt responsiveness of the other, he developed a contextualist understanding of psychoanalysis very close to intersubjectivity theory. No longer could the analyst claim a neutral role in the therapeutic process, claiming to be a blank screen for his patients' transferences. Instead, the observer became the observed, and the analyst was now implicated in all patient reactions. Thus, the selfobject function is a prime example of contextualism. The indivisibility of the observer and the observed in Kohut's theory is very similar to the early emphasis in intersubjectivity theory on the role that the theorist's subjectivity plays in the development of his or her theory. Kohut's subsequent development of his theory of narcissism and the narcissistic disorders was based on his understanding that his patients' suffering was due not to repressed drive derivatives in need of symbolization, sublimation, and transformation, and ultimately to impulses that the patient needed to give up in the service of maturation, but rather to experiences of a lack of developmentally necessary psychological nourishment. Thus, the concept of empathy that led to the concept of the selfobject and to the pathbreaking contextualization of narcissism is a unique contribution of Kohut to psychoanalysis. Another major contribution is the primacy of subjectivity. These three pillars of self psychology are central constituents of intersubjectivity theory. While Kohut's later (1977) "elevation of his psychology of narcissism to a metatheory of the total personality—a psychoanalytic psychology of the self—has created some knotty problems" (Stolorow et al., 1999, p. 384), as we shall see, he thereby left the road of recasting psychoanalysis as a pure psychology. In fact, the critique of intersubjectivity theory is based on Kohut's decontextualizing his own originally purely contextual definition of empathy. The intersubjective criticism is that Kohut left the empathic-introspective for an extrospective stance. "In Kohut's jump from phenomenology to ontology, self as a fluidly evolving dimension of experience taking form within an ongoing contextual matrix is replaced by self as an objectified, supraordinate, agentic entity, an ontic being equipped with poles and a tension arc, initiating actions to restore its own compromised cohesion. In this reification, which absolutized and universalized his clinical understandings, Kohut's hard-won contextualization of narcissism was partially undone, leading to an idolatry of psychological deficit, the doctrine of the deficits of the self. . . . The Cartesian isolated mind returns here in the Romantic vision of a pristine nuclear self, with its inherent preprogrammed design, awaiting a responsive milieu that will enable it to unfold" (Stolorow et al., 1999, p. 384). There are several points of criticism that need to be discussed regarding this quote. The main critique as it pertains to our trying to understand the stance of empathic inquiry is that by absolutizing a self with reified contents, such as ambitions and ideals, we lose the chance for the particular inquiry into a particular self-experience as it "is shaped at every point in the life cycle by the intersubjective context in which it crystallizes. Phenomenology keeps us ever contextual" (p. 384). The criticism is also leveled at the predominance of deficit experiences and at a too narrow focus on the selfobject dimension of experience and a view of transference that "neglect[s] and fail[s] to contextualize other important dimensions" (p. 384). It also addresses the seeming lack of mutual regulation. It is argued that Kohut was "reluctant to consider his framework a relational theory or a two-person theory, probably because he wanted to preserve its link to the intrapsychic [and thus Cartesian] tradition of Freudian psychoanalysis and to prevent its being characterized as an interpersonal or a social psychology" (p. 384). "If [one] looks at the evolution of Kohut's thought from *The Analysis of the Self* to *The Restoration of the Self,* [one] will see that he generalized important understandings of narcissism and the narcissistic personality disorder into a theory of the total personality and of the totality of analytic transferences. A generalized theory of narcissism will by definition leave out many other significant dimensions of experience and relatedness. Our intersubjective systems theory notes a few such dimensions, but in my view any such list will be incomplete. The possible dimensions of experience and of relatedness are, in principle, unlimited" (Stolorow, personal communication, 2004).

While this is a quite reasonable assessment and certainly is a theoretically stringent argument, contextualizing Kohut's contribution historically, with which I agree, I would like to add that in order for us to understand Kohut, a further historical contextualization is needed. It is necessary to point out the emotional harshness, the wall of rejection that Kohut was confronted with by international colleagues (some of whom would actually leave the room when he entered it), including his temporary exclusion from committees of his own institute. For an excellent and insightful description of the psychoanalytic fields that Kohut was embedded in, I recommend Charles Strozier's (2001) biography *Heinz Kohut: The Making of a Psychoanalyst*. If we understand his need to remain linked to the analytic world of his time—he *was* in close contact with the most renowned analysts, such as Anna Freud, to name just one—we can better understand his tremendous courage in risking the loss of his empathic milieu through the development of his revolutionary ideas.

Returning now to the intersubjectivist view: it is, as stated before but bearing repetition, that we argue neither for the intrapsychic nor for the interpersonal but rather for the *contextualization of the intrapsychic*. The "dichotomy between one-person and two-person psychologies is obsolete—reified, absolutized relics of the Cartesian bifurcation. The very phrase *two-person psychology* continues to embody an atomistic, isolated-mind philosophy in that two separated mental entities, two thinking things, are seen to bump into each other. We ought to speak instead of a contextual psychology, in which the individual and his or her world of personal experience are recognized as a subsystem of more encompassing relational or intersubjective suprasystems" (Stolorow et al., 1999, p. 384).

If we speak of a bias in favor of deficit psychology in self-psychological theory—and this is a critique also made by traditional psychoanalytic theorists, albeit for different reasons, and to which I will return at a later point—we again need to contextualize the contribution of self psychology to psychoanalysis in terms of a basic clinical attitude or sensitivity that this theory brought to psychoanalysis. For one, it was new indeed for psychoanalysts to speak of treatment offering "patients a developmental 'second chance' of a secure emotional attachment. Within such a bond they can experience the primary selfobject relatedness needed to develop a strong and valued sense of self" (Orange, 1995, p. 9). Moreover, "Self psychology describes the intersubjective field of treatment as a form of relatedness *in which an analyst or therapist can be unequivocally on the patient's side* . . . entering and remaining with the patient's self and relational experience" (p. 9). "In addition," and here I agree emphatically with Orange, "the attention self psychology gives to the effects of relational deprivation and of trauma concretely shapes my clinical thinking. No other psychoanalytic theory, I believe, focuses so directly on the emotional suffering and confusion of patients. No matter what level of abstraction or generality my theorizing may reach, self psychology keeps me emotionally close to patients" (p. 9)—not to view patients as attempting primarily to manipulate the therapist or somehow malignantly draw him or her into some form of role enactment for secondary gains, not to view patients antagonistically, and not to second-guess their "true motives" but instead to keep their emotional suffering, even if all appearances are to the contrary, as our touchstone for understanding is crucial for this form of clinical sensitivity. Not to lose sight of suffering and deprivation can be our guiding light when we are in danger of being engulfed by the darkness of hateful or empty despair.

A COMPARISON OF EMPATHY AND INSTROSPECTIVE-EMPATHIC INQUIRY

Let me now focus on some of the similarities and differences between Kohut's concept of empathy and the intersubjective concept of empathic-introspective inquiry, both of which address the process of psychoanalytic knowing. Both concepts differ from Cartesian isolated-mind thinking of traditional psychoanalysis that was associated with a technical rationality and an objectivist epistemology. As was stated before, "such a position envisions the mind in isolation, radically separated from an external reality that it either accurately apprehends or misperceives. Analysts embracing an objectivist epistemology presume to have privileged access both to the essence of the patient's reality and to the objective truths that this reality, in form of transference, distorts" (Stolorow et al., 1999, p. 385). In contrast, the intersubjectivists conceptualize the process of psychoanalytic knowing as a form of *perspectivalism* or *perspectival realism*. This stance does not presume that the analyst's subjective reality is more true than the patient's or that we can directly know the subjective world of the patient; instead, we can only "approximate this reality from within the particularized scope of the analyst's own perspective" (p. 385). This is very similar to Kohut's claim that we "can only describe what we see within the framework of what we have done to see it" (Kohut, 1984b, p. 91) and to his conviction in "the relativity of our perceptions of reality . . . the relativity of the framework of ordering concepts that shape our observations and explanations" (Kohut, 1982, p. 400).

In his efforts to define empathy as a scientific method of observation, Kohut (1980) stated that "empathy (vicarious introspection) is in essence *neutral and objective*, it is not in its essence subjective" (p. 483). He described empathy as an attempt at an accurate assessment of the inner life of a person, not to be confused with or guided primarily by sympathy or compassion. So in trying to counter the sentimentality and mysticism critique, he retreated from his own contextualist stance that the observer is the observed and unwittingly decontextualized empathy. Clearly, empathy cannot be seen as a neutral stance for several reasons. First, the emphasis on emotional responsiveness in facilitating the development of selfhood is part of a theoretical belief system. Second, as Kohut (1980) himself pointed out, the patient will also not experience empathy as a neutral stance, seeing as it meets deep longings to be understood. Or, conversely, a patient may react with fear, irritation, or anger to empathy because it may reawaken encapsulated selfobject longings that are experienced as threatening if they expose the patient to the risk of being failed once again. Third—and this is the main criticism that intersubjectivity theory points out—the idea that one isolated mind, the analyst, can enter and directly gaze on another isolated mind, the patient, leaving his or her psychological world outside and viewing the patient's inner experience with preconceptionless eyes, is not possible. "This doctrine of immaculate perception entails a denial of the inherently intersubjective nature of analytic understanding, to which the analyst's subjectivity makes an ongoing, unavertable contribution" (Stolorow et al., 1999, p. 386). Rather than attempting to be objective and to banish our subjectivity, we need to decenter (Atwood and Stolorow, 1984; Piaget, 1974) by becoming reflectively aware of how our personal organizing principles are influencing our analytic understandings.

PERSPECTIVAL REALISM AND THE RISK OF RELATEDNESS

Perspectival realism is a stance that has been influenced, among others, by the hermeneutic ontology of Hans-Georg Gadamer (1991). Borrowing Gadamer's view (concerning text interpretation) that we need to stop looking for meaning solely in the mind of the patient (author) and rather to seek it in the dialogic interplay of hermeneutic process, Orange (2002) writes that "understanding emerges not from immersion in the mind of the other, but from the conversation between and among those who seek understanding while examining one's own prejudices and welcoming alternative points of view. We are never in the mind of the other, nor are we ever outside the conversation. The conversation, as Gadamer has often remarked, is not one that we have chosen; rather, it seems to choose us and challenges us to be changed by it. In such a view, there is no way for the analyst to be 'accurately empathic' or to be outside the relational experience enough to be a good judge of what the patient is doing to others, including the analyst" (Orange, 2002, p. 694).

The fact that the focus of intersubjectivity theory is not on the isolated mind but on the larger system created by the interplay of the subjective worlds of patient and analyst (or of child and caregiver) fits exactly with the epistemological stance of perspectival realism: "the only truth or reality to which psychoanalysis provides access is the subjective organization of experience understood in an intersubjective context" (Orange, 1995, p. 61). "The perspectivalist attitude has a profound effect on the *ambience* of the psychoanalytic situation" (Stolorow et al., 2002, p. 103, emphasis added). I would like to address this point first from the standpoint of the risk of relatedness for the therapist: it is equally relieving and anxiety-provoking. To understand that one does not possess the God's-eye view (Putnam, 1990), that is, that no one can have all perspectives of a situation, can be a tremendous relief. Understanding a priori how limited the slice of the pie of reality is that we have access to, because our understanding of anything is always just an interpretation, limited by the historicity of our own subjectivity and our "prejudices" (Gadamer, 1991), takes the burden of omniscience from us. This omniscience can be fueled either by an overestimation of ourselves or more likely, in my experience, by the pressure that comes with the therapeutic territory of playing such an immensely important role in the second developmental chance of our patients. While this importance is certainly vital for our sense of being engaged in a meaningful task and thus a source of sustenance for our lives, I know of few therapists who do not also experience this responsibility as a considerable weight to be shouldered. Somewhat akin to the tightrope walker, using a pole to maintain balance, one walks a thin line between the weight and the inspiration. To once again paraphrase Gadamer (1991), he thought that we shouldn't attempt to exclude our subjectivity from the process of understanding. On the contrary, an authentic hermeneutic approach entails emphasizing the prejudices of our subjectivity, thereby stripping them of their extreme character and thus allowing a clearer perception of what is foreign to us. It is not neutrality that allows us to be receptive to the foreignness of what we try to understand but rather the awareness of our preconceived notions. The very familiarity of our own opinions lets the foreignness of the other appear in bold relief. As mentioned earlier, we can acquire a taste for the foreignness by always expecting that the other person can teach us something. So we are able to change our predilection to be tempted to view our opinion as a fair account of the whole and thus turn the fact that our limited perspective leaves us likely to often be wrong into a positive attitude of curiosity. This playfulness can, in turn, balance the weight of responsibility. Peircian ([1905] 1931–1935) fallibilism, which asks us to wear the coats of our theories and perceptions lightly, always being willing to shrug them off in favor of being taught something new, guarantees that we remain open and receptive to the perspectives of others. Nonetheless, the idea that we should know what's what seems to have an intangible hold on us, and the notion that we could give this attitude up seems to be a siren call into the structureless chaos of relatedness, which we would prefer to avoid by staying strapped to the mast of the isolated mind. What are the dangers of not knowing, which feels so much like losing control?

We said earlier that the function of the isolated mind was to avoid "Cartesian anxiety," or the unbearable embeddedness of being. If we approach each session with a hermeneutic, perspectivist attitude, are we saying that there is no reality, that there is no truth, no internal or external? No, because that would be to confuse intersubjective contextualism with postmodern nihilism or relativism. No, because we are not taking refuge in an attitude that says that every framework and every interpretation is as good as the next, as in relativism, as if anything goes (Orange, 1995). Obviously, pragmatically some ideas will be better than others in facilitating the psychoanalytic process. Instead, we are speaking of relativity to *context*: there is reality, but our knowing of it will be limited by perspective and culture (Stolorow et al., 2002). As for truth, we have to distinguish between questions of meaning and those of truth. We are not speaking of truth as corresponding to facts; rather, meanings will arise in the intersubjective field of the analyst's and the patient's subjectivities, including the differences of perspectives, and can be ascertained only within that context. So, intersubjectivity theory claims that statements about reality and truth or falsehood "are meaningful only within systems, and that conversation is required for meanings to become apparent. The process of making sense together is what we call *understanding*" (Stolorow et al., 2002, pp. 116–117). "And here we arrive at a fundamental tenet of our psychoanalytic contextualism: Truth is dialogic, crystallizing from the inescapable interplay of observer and observed" (Stolorow et al., 1999, p. 387). "The claim that all psychoanalytic understanding is interpretive means there are no decontextualized absolutes or universals, no neutral or objective analysts, no immaculate perceptions, no God's-eye views (Putnam, 1990) of anything or anyone. This fallibilistic attitude encourages us to hold lightly not only theory but any particular meaning in the co-created experience in the intersubjective field of treatment" (Stolorow et al., 2002, p. 76). So, what is relieving is that our horizons are expanded by multiple possibilities of meaning, and we are freed from the "tyranny of fixed horizons and frozen meaning" (Orange, 2002, p. 693). The multiplicity, fluidity, and context-sensitivity of meanings can, however, also cause anxiety.

I would like to return to the experience of felt danger, of losing control if we embrace intersubjectivity theory. I said earlier that we object to giving up our sense of omniscience. *Omniscience* is a strong word, open to a critique of pathological overestimation. But I mean to use it descriptively as a felt experience that we probably keep hidden from ourselves. Which therapist in his or her right mind would claim omniscience? So let us examine this state more closely. If, as Gadamer claims, the conversation chooses us and challenges us to be changed by it and if we are never outside the conversation, never outside the relational experience, or, as Orange (2002) puts it so succinctly, "there is no outside" (p. 699), then I think we could experience this as a threat to our *experience* of distinctness—a threat to our experience of self and other boundaries, to our sense of selfhood, an experience of being like a drop in the ocean, making us feel disappearingly small, claustrophobically lost in the immense sea of being, as if, to use yet another metaphor, the universe were a huge lung breathing us. The question is, Do we welcome the experience of being part of the fabric of the universe, or do we revolt with a feeling of "let me out of here, I want to be me"? We return now to the basic tenets of the intersubjective philosophy of life described in chapter 1: can we escape our existential vulnerabilities by claiming to be apart from all that sustains us?

In psychotherapeutic treatment, "once we make the radical shift to embodied experience (not presumed drive-based motivations) as the subject matter of psychoanalytic theory and practice, we are immediately confronted with the impossibility of deciding to whom the experience belongs, in the sense of an inner possession. To be a subject means to possess a perspective, whether rigid or more flexible, that organizes my experiential world, not as an object, but as a system further embedded within . . . human forms of life" (Orange, 2002, p. 693). "We are always living within such systems and can only pretend to be outside" (p. 694).

Orange writes about the languages and communicative systems in which we live but which can also be applied to the entirety of lived experience, including the psychotherapeutic process.

THE MISLEADING DICHOTOMY OF INTERNAL AND EXTERNAL

We have addressed the issues of reality and truth and turn now to the issue of internal and external to conclude our examination of the intersubjective stance of empathic inquiry. In this view of empathic inquiry, we are not entering from the outside into the mind or the experience of the patient; we are not seeking objectively verifiable truth. Rather, we are living within the experiential world that we create together with the patient and in which we try to arrive through communitarian dialogue at an approximation of the patient's subjective reality. In this clinical sensibility, if we get stuck or find ourselves in any kind of predicament with the patient, we've gotten stuck together, and we need to ask ourselves and our patients, How did we manage this? The rejection of the inner–outer bifurcation should not be misconstrued as a rejection of the inner in favor of the outer. In her seminal paper "There Is No Outside: Empathy and Authenticity in Psychoanalytic Process," Orange (2002) reviews Merton Gill's (1994) examination of the divisive and misleading bifurcation in terms of several dichotomies: internal and external, subject and object, conflict and deficit. Gill makes the point that "all the forms of dichotomy can be seen as differentiating schools of thought in psychoanalysis" (Orange, 2002, p. 697), and Orange notes that each school values one side of the dichotomy as more fundamentally real.

Gill begins with Freud, who started the inner–outer debate in psychoanalysis by heavily emphasizing one side or the other of the nature–nurture, constitution–environment argument, only to contradict and reverse his position, showing his understanding that things were not so one-sided or clear-cut. In Gill's (1994) view, close to the intersubjective understanding, "otherness is not a thing-in-itself, but rather an aspect of continually self-organizing experience within relational systems" (p. 696). Gill retains the terms *subject* and *object* but redefines *transference* and *countertransference* as a product of both participants. Gill offers a solution to the dichotomy by stating that "the internal plays a role in shaping the external and the external plays a role in shaping the internal and applies this principle to the relationship between transference and countertransference. Positing a division between internal and external is misleading unless it is recognized that each contributes to shaping the other" (p. 27). Gill notes the similarity between his view and the interplay of subjective worlds in the intersubjective field. Finally, Gill examines the conflict–deficit dichotomy, citing classical analysis as relentlessly criticizing self psychology for neglecting internally generated conflict and having a bias in favor of deficits presumably caused by external factors. (For a discussion of this critique of self psychology, see Jaenicke, 1993.) His solution is once again to note that conflicts and deficits do not exist alone; rather, they create each other. In reviewing the analytic schools, he shows which side of the dichotomy they favor: for Freudians and Kleinians, the internal, the conflictual, and the subjective are primary; the external is secondary. Self psychologists emphasize developmental deficits and reject drive theory–generated conflict. Interpersonalists have a bias for the external here and now, viewing anything else as secondary and defensive: "The external forms the internal, more than vice-versa. . . . It is surely useful to point out that inner and outer, subject and object (or in other theories subjectivity and intersubjectivity), conflict and deficit, are mutually defining and inextricable from each other" (Orange, 2002, p. 697).

Orange (2002) points out that the basic problem of these bifurcations is that we can be misled to forget the metaphorical quality of concepts, to believe, for instance, that we could understand inner and outer as separate states outside the intersubjective systems they are embedded in. It can mislead us to thinking "that it is possible to describe" what is going on around here, "what the patient is doing to me, or I to the patient, as if one or both of us could momentarily stand outside the system we constitute together" (p. 698). Orange continues by stating that "in a Winnicottian spirit . . . there is no such thing as a patient, that there is only a patient within the context of the analyst's care, and conversely that there is no such thing as an analyst, but only an analyst for and with this particular patient" (p. 698). In terms of clinical consequences, perspectival realism, or the stance of sustained empathic inquiry, leads us to always question what is or isn't going on in our particular relationship that is creating a particular feeling in the patient. "The question is not here-and-now versus there-and-then, nor is it conflict versus deficit. Rather, it is recognizing with Gadamer that everything is past-loaded, that we converse and inquire within a conversation that is in part created by us, but within which we find ourselves. We are inside the conversation, which is itself always further embedded in larger cultural (political, racial, sexual, and so on) contexts. There is no outside" (pp. 698–699).

EMPATHY VERSUS AUTHENTICITY?

If we can embrace the idea that there is no outside, we can also answer the issue of whether empathy and authenticity are opposites: does empathy—following the patient's emotional perspective closely—require us to be inauthentic or dishonest, or, conversely, does being authentic mean that we distance ourselves from our patients? Actually, there is no choice because in being empathic we cannot abandon our own subjectivity, our own ongoing organizing of experience. Likewise, in being authentic we cannot distance ourselves from our patients in the sense that we could refer to a perspective outside the conversation or system that we find ourselves in. We could and do decide to put aside a particular reaction we have toward a patient, such as feeling hurt in the face of a patient's expression of angry disappointment toward us, in favor of following an authentic analytic ideal we have of wanting to explore the meaning of the patient's feeling; in so doing, we are not being dishonest. Or we may feel that it is facilitating for the therapeutic process to participate within the system in a confrontative manner; this would not mean we are being unempathic. Orange (2002, p. 699) quotes Aron (1996, p. 194): "relational theory does not dictate a particular form of analytic activity as much as it insists on the recognition of inevitable and continuous participation." "Empathy, I believe, is emotional knowledge gained by participation in a shared reality" (Orange, 1995, p. 21).

WHAT IS AN EMPATHIC INTERVENTION?

I am frequently asked to give an example of a self-psychological, empathic intervention. As an intersubjectivist, with roots in self psychology, I like to propose, much like I have often heard the prominent self psychologists Anna and Paul Ornstein say, "show me the text, tell me the therapeutic exchange." Empathy, as a mode of understanding, is context-bound. It cannot, for instance, as is still misunderstood, be reduced to a so-called supportive mirroring function. Nor is it to be confused with Rogerian client-centered therapy. Stolorow (1976) pointed out the valuable contributions of client-centered therapy and some of the similarities of the approaches, especially with regard to clinical sensibility and to treating the narcissistic dimension of the transference. There are, however, also vast differences. Aside from those that can be found in the theoretical and clinical analytic literature, I would like to name two that are relevant to this discussion: We do not operationalize love, warmth, and appreciation, much less suggest it as a technique, nor can empathy be reduced to paraphrasing the patient. For instance, for a patient who is experientially on extremely shaky ground, empathy may guide us to say, "I believe you will get better." This is another example of concretistic empathy. As always, it takes into account the appropriate assessment of where the patient is on the developmental continuum as well as our understanding of how that fits into the intersubjective field. For other patients, empathy may guide us to offer interpretations based less on the need for tight acknowledgment of a merger state and instead to suggest a more symbolic interpretation, such as "You need me to tell you that you will get better" or "If I told you that you will get better, I would be aligning myself with that part of you that is doubtful," or "Yes, you feel great despair." The traditional view, one that lends itself to regarding only those interpretations that are given on a symbolic level as analytic (originally the theoretical reasoning was to avoid gratification), may leave out the contextual assessment of the patient in terms of development and the therapeutic field. These hypothetical examples are invalid in the sense that they do not originate in the specific intersubjective field of a particular therapeutic dyad. I have allowed myself this slight decontexualization in order to highlight the idea that any intervention is analytic—within the ethical boundaries of our profession—as long as it reflects the specific empathic understanding of an intersubjective field. Empathy leaves us unlimited possibilities in terms of our interventions, as many as there are meanings to be discovered. This includes the possibility of confrontation, if it is called for empathically and facilitates the intersubjective process. Perhaps Kohut's (1984) remarks on confrontation have been somewhat misleading concerning this issue and in this sense have contributed to the misunderstanding of empathy. He believed that life itself usually offers our patients enough confrontative fields and that we need not add to them in therapy, only to contradict himself in the case of a patient whose reckless driving was endangering his life. To this patient, Kohut felt impelled—in another example of concretistic empathy—to say words to the effect of "You are behaving like an idiot!"

I would like to end this exploration of the intersubjective stance of empathic-introspective inquiry with a quote from Gadamer (1991): "The person with understanding does not know and judge as one who stands apart and unaffected; but rather, as one united by a specific bond with the other, he thinks with the other and undergoes the situation with him" (p. 288).

3

Affects: The Paradigm Shift in Psychoanalysis

> The psychoanalyst knows that the forces he works with are of the most explosive kind.
>
> (S. Freud)

> All torment, trouble, wonder and amazement inhabits here. Some heavenly power guide us out of this fearful country.
>
> (Shakespeare, *The Tempest*)

"Vous ne voyez pas une chaise avant vous" ("You wouldn't see a chair, even if it stood right in front of you"), my first French analyst admonished me. "Never neglect the obvious," he added somewhat more kindly in answer to my scowl. Not one to neglect his own advice, he once asked my permission to eat his "poulet froid" (cold chicken) when he hadn't had the time to have lunch. He was a Jungian analyst by training and a fierce individualist. Lest one get the wrong idea, I have had the privilege of also being treated by an orthodox German and an intersubjective American analyst. The one thing they had in common was that all three were phenomenologists. It was, however, my French analyst, a compassionate and intelligent man, who was the first person to suggest I'd make a good analyst—a notion that I found ludicrous beyond words at the time, thinking I wouldn't be caught dead imprisoned behind a couch listening to people's woes all day. My heroes being Bob Dylan and Mick Jagger, I couldn't imagine a less desirable profession. Nonetheless, not only did the seed he had sown eventually bear fruit, as I have lived and breathed psychoanalysis most of my life, but his advice to never neglect the obvious is a lesson I continue to learn some 40 years later.

The "obvious" in psychotherapy is affect. Still under the sway of being the "talking cure," we are often in danger of being seduced by the content of our patients' productions before we even ascertain what can be found in their faces or heard in the tone of their voices, that is, to understand the main feeling they show us at any given time. We do not see the proverbial forest (feeling) for all the trees (content). But before we can turn to the clinical consequences of placing affect in the center of our therapeutic attention, we need to explore the centrality that affect has for psychoanalytic practice and theory.

WHO ON EARTH MADE ME CHOOSE THIS JOB?[1]

In discussing the role of emotions, or affect,[2] I would like to begin with an imagistic, descriptive approach of what it is like to practice psychoanalysis. Psychotherapy is about the very specific mix of two people: what happens when you expose each other intimately over long periods of time? Psychoanalysis is about emotions and emotions are emotional.[3] It's like putting certain ingredients into a pot and then experiencing—and trying to explain—how they interact. The therapist is also in there getting cooked and transformed, all the while trying to stay focused in terms of what it means for the patient. The risk of relatedness is that you can understand what it's like to be the patient only if you give yourself up to the process of involvement. No matter who you encounter, there's no escape from the beauty and the horror of emotional entanglement. The inevitability of being touched in ways that we don't choose voluntarily—except in that we chose this profession—the daily imperative to be open to the encounter, means that we can never predict the combustability of the emotional brew that evolves. "The analyst at work cannot be protected from the anxieties (and feelings) transmitted by means of either his technique or his scientific knowledge; the quality of understanding is personally endured" (Maccio, 1992, pp. 89–90). A colleague, shortly before his vacation, once put it this way: "I need a break from exposure, I feel like I have a sunburn."

"Anyone who is going to see a patient tomorrow should, at some point, experience fear. In every consulting room there ought to be two rather frightened people: the patient and the psychoanalyst. If they are not, one wonders why they are bothering to find out what everyone knows" (Bion, 1990, pp. 4–5). Bion is referring to how disturbing it is to approach the unconscious. However, my point is a broader one having to do with the intersubjective nature of human relatedness and the analytic encounter in general and the "inherently complex and relational nature of emotional life" (Orange, 1995, p. 95) in particular.

If it seems that I am "kvetching"[4] about the trials and tribulations of being a therapist, that I am biased in favor of the risks involved for the analyst, then this is certainly true in the sense that I start with my own subjective experience, and it is true in the sense that the risk of relatedness is a major theme of this book. However, my main intention is to address the aspect of mutuality—including the risks for both participants—inherent in the analytic relationship. On the one hand, the seeming bias is an attempt to redress an imbalance inherent in the theory and sensibility of traditional psychoanalysis, which has already been extensively dealt with by many prominent contemporary authors (e.g., Aron, 1996; Mitchell, 1988; Momigliano and Robutti, 1992; Orange, 1995; Renik, 1993; Stolorow, Brandchaft, and Atwood, 1987). On the other hand, as I've mentioned before, there is another imbalance needing attention: the taboo concerning the exploration of the emotions of the analyst in terms of the extent of our involvement, our frailty, our needs, the relativity of our ability to know and to heal, in short, the limitations of our power and the emotional cost of being a therapist. A further issue that has been neglected but most recently addressed by Bodansky (2004) and Lachmann (2003) is the use of humor and, I would add, the role of joyful exuberance in the psychotherapeutic process.

In this chapter, I attempt to address these issues through the prism of the central role of emotions in psychoanalytic practice and theory. If we view the analytic relationship as the meeting between two equally involved people "trying to understand each other through their common emotional substance" (Momigliano and Robutti, 1992, p. 1), then analysis is seen as a "natural process, in the sense that it is our nature to seek a relation with others. During analysis an emotional developmental process—which previous, insufficiently welcoming relationships have distorted or blocked—is resumed" (pp. 3–4). We are then creating a space "in which something emerges of which neither of the two is any longer the master" (p. 8). Not to fear, I am not propagating "structureless chaos," a critique of intersubjectivity theory dealt with before (see also Stolorow, Atwood, and Brandchaft, 1994). Rather, I would like to make an observation, one that I am at pains to remember, much like the chair, lest I fall over it: it is, after all, a *relationship* that we enter into with each patient, albeit one structured by the therapeutic purpose both of us pursue. However, I can think of no other profession where both are so intricately linked. When you look at the rippled surface of a lake, what is it that you're seeing, the wind or the water?

Momigliano and Robutti's (1992) language is very close to the language of intersubjectivity theory, where we speak of the intersubjective fields—we need to add the past and the future to the present field—the indissoluble units from which emotional "truths" emerge dialogically. This view leads to a very different clinical sensibility and environment: "The oracular, sphinx-like, shamanic style of the analyst is toned down and the psychoanalytic arrogance disappears . . . [and] the stereotyped solemnity" (Momigliano and Robutti, 1992, p. 8) is no longer seen as a sine qua non for establishing a transference neurosis.

While I have disagreements with the concept of the "real relationship" propagated by Gestalt therapists, I can understand their what-else-is-new shrug of the shoulders concerning this point. Renik (2005) went so far as to describe psychoanalysis as on the wane, if not to say on its deathbed, in America, if it continues to neglect the intersubjective, emotional nature of the therapeutic encounter. Given the vitality of new directions in psychoanalysis, I can't agree with this dire forecast, but his critique, which centers largely on the attempt to leave out the subjectivity of the analyst in the equation of mutuality in the intersubjective field and the neglect of the depth of the emotional involvement of both therapeutic partners, needs to be taken seriously. Renik (1993) makes a plea for us to revise our theories of technique so as to make it "unnecessary for us to ask ourselves, in vain, not to be passionately and irrationally involved in our everyday clinical work" (p. 570). Similarly, Mitchell (1988) states that unless we enter into and emotionally find ourselves within the patient's relational matrix, unless we are charmed, shaped, antagonized, and frustrated by the patient's entreaties, defenses, and projections, the treatment will remain flat. Bion saw the analytic relationship as symmetrical to the extreme in his view of the therapeutic dyad as two frightened people, describing the patient as the analyst's best colleague, but asymmetrical in the sense that the analyst is wholly responsible for the development of the analytic process. He or she is responsible but shares the risks with the patient.

I have prefaced the discussion of the role of affects in psychoanalysis with another description of the intersubjective nature of the psychotherapeutic process because for a long time, beginning with Freud, emotions were treated atomistically as primary affective states preceding relational and intersubjective experience and "as mere epiphenomena, as derivative from those essential motivators, the instinctual drives" (Orange, 1995, p. 89). My purpose here is not to offer a comprehensive overview of the development of affect theory in psychoanalysis, as Krystal (1988), Orange (1995), and Spezzano (1993) have already so aptly done, but to attempt to explain why the Cartesian isolated-mind view of affects still maintains an understandable but deleterious hold on psychotherapeutic practice. It is my thesis that this is an outcome of the risks of relatedness inherent in our work.

FREUD'S AFFECT THEORY: PSYCHOLOGICAL DISCOVERIES AND METAPSYCHOLOGICAL MUSEUMS

As Spezzano (1993) has pointed out, Freud's theories, on any issue, were always complex and contradictory, but he did have a theory of affects, whether one agrees with it or not. "He provided a comprehensive account of the role of sexual excitement, rage, anxiety, and guilt in psychic life . . . a useful, if not comprehensive account, of the pain of separation and the affective states of mourning and melancholia through which we experience loss. He clearly and consistently specified sexual excitement, rage, anxiety, and guilt as the fundamental categories of human meaning and, therefore, of human experience" (pp. 82–83). For Freud, the existential motivators are the instinctual drives, and it is the drives that generate affective states. As mentioned earlier, the problems that arise from Freudian theory are due to the discrepancy between his clinical and his metapsychological theories. In terms of his metapsychology, Freud's reduction of human motivation to sexual excitement and rage can be understood as an attempt to scientize human emotion.

The difference between psychoanalysis in Freud's time and our own is much more radical than is generally acknowledged; we cannot understand Freud apart from the cultural and historical context in which he lived (Mitchell, 1993). In this context, the psychoanalytic goal of removing symptoms by making the unconscious conscious and by attaining rational control over the drives made sense. In Freud's scientific understanding, the patient's unconscious fantasies, leading to irrationality and distortions, could be corrected by the analyst's more objective knowledge. It wasn't that Freud didn't understand his patient's subjective meanings and values but rather that they were of secondary importance in comparison to a rational, objective understanding of the intrapsychic fate of the drive derivatives. Today we would place less emphasis on a rational reworking of infantile wishes and more on helping the patient feel vital and valuable (Mitchell, 1993). The focus of contemporary psychoanalysis is less on renunciation and insight—concepts that were intricately linked for Freud—and more on the expansion, confirmation and reconciliation of subjective experience. What the patient needs is not so much clarification and rational insight but rather "a sustained experience of being seen, personally engaged, and, basically valued and cared about" (p. 25). If for Freud the rational awareness of sexual and aggressive fantasies and their subjugation to realistic control were pivotal for mental health, contemporary psychoanalysis focuses on the difficulties of the patient to comprehend the nature of his or her experience and to feel that it is real, important, and meaningful.

Therefore, a basic shift has occurred in psychoanalysis in our understanding about what the patient needs: the experience and development of meaning and authenticity have replaced insight and renunciation. In our view, *meaning* replaces the drives as the central organizing motivational principle in human experience. Understanding our subjective emotions as they develop and become crystallized in our intersubjective fields is the medium through which we attain meaning and authenticity. It is not that conflicts over sexual and aggressive feelings have been disregarded; rather, they have become deuniversalized, relocated, and recontextualized within a relational model. The basic, paradigmatic shift in psychoanalysis from the primacy of the drives to the primacy of affects—that is, subjective emotional experience—has led to a contextualist understanding of all aspects of human psychological life (Stolorow, Atwood, and Orange, 2002).

Orange cites Aristoteles when she criticizes the assumption that the goal of life is to attain pleasurable affect states and avoid unpleasant states. This view ignores that pleasure and pain are byproducts of human activities and not goals in themselves; as such, they are qualities of experience, not things in themselves (Orange, 1995). The oversimplification involved in reducing emotions to states or things is a concretization itself. "The concretization principle also provides an explanation for the ubiquitous tendency to reify and substantialize the products of human thought, transforming linguistic concepts and abstract ideas into an illusory, symbolic architecture lending concrete substance to organizations of personal, subjective reality" (Atwood and Stolorow, 1984, p. 120).

Clinically—and here the discrepancy to Freud's metapsychology becomes apparent—according to Spezzano (1993) the most radical of Freud's reformulations was that the truth that is most important in a person's psychological struggle to survive is not a scientific or a hermeneutic truth but an affective truth. It was Freud who opened the way with his discovery of the unconscious and the development of his psychoanalytic method to the uncoerced discourse between two people necessary for the search for affective truth that psychoanalysis seeks.

TRADITIONALISM: A HINDRANCE FOR NEW PSYCHOANALYTIC DEVELOPMENTS

However, Freud was also a child of his time, and so is his metapsychology which, as I hope to demonstrate, still holds sway over too much of today's clinical practice and sensibility and which entails a major stumbling block in the psychoanalytic commmunity's ability to move ahead with the integration of its own innovations. The questions, therefore, are these: Why is it so difficult for psychoanalysis to acknowledge and integrate the truly revolutionary developments of past decades? Why is there still a tendency to mitigate innovations as mere technical refinements or expansions of Freudian thinking, to implicitly oppose them as a form of heresy, or to incorporate new ideas, only to present them as reinterpretations of Freud? Clearly, Freud's monumental work anticipates many of today's problems, but it does not offer the discoveries made by contemporary psychoanalysis. The identity-enhancing love affair with Freud and psychoanalytic traditions is understandable, as it allows analysts to benefit from its founder's authority and genius (Mitchell, 1993).

Nonetheless, the adhesiveness of traditional psychoanalytic thinking has resulted in an inability to acknowledge the radical difference between the way psychoanalysis is practiced today and the way it was practiced 100 years ago. The omnipresent question of whether a concept or clinical activity is analytic—and here the issue of lineage remains relevant—still prevails over whether they are therapeutically helpful. It is as if the acceptance of innovations is synonymous with a shameful rejection of the founder of psychoanalysis. So one finds oneself emphasizing the discontinuities rather than the continuities in psychoanalysis (Mitchell, 1993). A diffuse anxiety remains that one may have inadvertently excluded oneself from the mainstream of psychoanalysis—a science that was invented and driven by Freud's restless and innovative spirit but that has nonetheless undergone enormous changes. To summarize, exaggerated traditionalism has impeded the acknowledgment and integration of new psychoanalytic developments. Freud himself once was reported to have commented to Theodor Reik: "Moi, je ne suis pas une Freudiste" ("I myself am not a Freudian") (Reik, 1954, p. 513, cited in Dufresne, 2003, p. 70). To paraphrase Nietzsche's Zarathustra, one pays the teacher little respect by forever remaining his student (Dufresne, 2003).

One could raise the question whether I am creating a straw man with these thoughts on traditionalism. My impression is that psychoanalysis, especially in America, is generally quite vital. The recalcitrance toward change I have described, however, still holds true both on an international level as well as on the much more subtle level of clinical attitudes and sensibilities. Therefore, I would like to describe—in broad brush strokes—how our new understanding of science and psychoanalysis has changed our profession: the dwindling belief in the transformative power of reason, the shift from clarity to ambiguity and imagination, from one Truth to many truths, from objectivity to subjectivity, from universal drives to subjective emotional experience, from the closed system of intrapsychic mechanisms to the mutual regulation of the intersubjective field, from a decontextualized view of interpretations as expansions of consciousness to relational events. In the following, I try to shed some light on the adhesiveness of traditionalism.

THE HISTORICAL CONTEXT OF TRADITIONALISM

Why do analysts who subscribe to new developments constantly feel pursued by Freud's shadow? Perhaps this is a transgenerational inheritance of Freud's own struggles to protect the purity and core identity of the young science of psychoanalysis against a hostile social and scientific community. To preserve the core identity, Freud demanded an explicit identification with his central theses. Those who disagreed left or were banished from his inner circle. As a result, many of its most creative talents were marginalized, and psychoanalysis fragmented into competing belief systems. Altmeyer (2004) described the many belief systems, each with their own identity and language, as a Tower of Babel in need of deconstruction. Recently, there have been some hopeful signs that psychoanalysis is no longer paralyzed by the need to find one "truth" or by the issue of analytic versus nonanalytic. The analytic schools seem to have begun to recognize the quasi-religious bias of their belief systems and to focus more on the theoretical validity and practical usefulness of their concepts. It is not my intention to mitigate the differences between psychoanalytic concepts, which need acknowledgment and discussion. I am making a plea for a discourse that allows us to keep useful concepts and leave anachronisms behind and that doesn't regard new developments as a threat. The attention given to the patient's resources and not only their pathology as well as the equal importance allotted to perceiving and working with the implicit and not only the explicit aspects of relatedness seem to be examples of a renewed ability to undo splits in psychoanalysis and allow new developments. I do not agree with the almost routinely broadcast announcements of the death of psychoanalysis. The only cause for concern can be found in an underestimation of the role of emotions and relatedness.

I would like to come full circle now and attempt to point out those issues in which the legacy of Freud's metapsychology as anchored in his affect theory find expression in our present-day problems with the risks of relatedness in the psychotherapeutic process. Perhaps this exploration can shed some light on why it is still difficult for many analysts to overcome Freud's injunction to disregard psychoanalytic innovations for fear of banishment from the "inner circle" and why psychoanalysis still feels impelled to maintain discoveries made a century ago.

AFFECTS: ENERGY TRANSFORMATION VERSUS INFORMATION PROCESSING

In Krystal's (1988) seminal book on affects, *Integration and Self-Healing: Affect, Trauma, Alexithymia,* he describes Freud's view of emotions as reflecting the physiological and psychiatric attitudes of his age. It was burdened with a mind–body dichotomy and a mechanistic attitude toward the bodily processes. The result of thinking of mental functions as a reflex arc was a view of emotions as discharge phenomena. Throughout the development of his affect theories—whether as inborn drive-discharge channels, as safety valves, as indicators of drive tension, or as signals (Spezzano, 1993)—affects remained related to drive cathexis. As such, they also remained "discharge" phenomena.

The "discharge" metaphor did not origininate with Freud but was a theater metaphor (catharsis) where it was used to describe a subjective experience of relief concerning emotional states or wishes one wanted to be rid of. "Many of the metaphors that have become part of psychoanalytic lore involve the idea of elimination as the true meaning of the idea of affect 'expression.' All of them are related to the continuing use of the model of energy transformation, instead of information processing" (Krystal, 1988, p. 77). Anal analogies are also in common usage in everyday language, such as speaking of "shitty feelings."

Rather than being seen as a quality of all experience, affect is seen in this view as a discrete, time-limited, peak experience, an explosion experienced as an attack on self-experience and the other. Stolorow and Atwood (1992) have defined the essence of trauma as unbearable affect originating not in the drives but in the misregulation of the intersubjective field. "Pain is not pathology. It is the absence of adequate attunement and responsiveness to the child's painful emotional reactions that renders them unendurable and thus a source of traumatic states and psychopathology" (p. 54).

I will describe how intersubjectivity theory views affect at a later point. My purpose here is to reflect on those aspects of affect theory that I believe have outlived their theoretical and clinical usefulness but that continue to exert their influence on therapeutic practice because, as I hope to show, they are related to the issue of the risk of relatedness. However, in order to "discharge" some of the tension, I will insert this summative quotation from intersubjectivity theory: "Unlike drives, which originate deep within the interior of a Cartesian isolated mind, affect is something that from birth onward is regulated, or misregulated, within ongoing relational systems. Therefore locating affect at its center automatically entails a radical contextualization of virtually all aspects of human psychological life" (Stolorow et al., 2002, p. 11).

Returning now to the theme of affect as elimination or as information processing, if affect is viewed not primarily as a derivative of an inborn, intrapsychic phenomenon but as a contextualization of an intrapsychic experience, that is, as an intersubjective phenomenon, then it is easier to answer the question of why affects and their interrelations were so long disregarded in psychoanalysis and found no place of their own within metapsychology.

According to Freudian metapsychology, the drives are always operative and are therefore always producing the affects of sexual excitement and of rage, or they are in a dialectic tension with anxiety and guilt. How can affect then not be viewed as an attempt to rid oneself of troublesome feelings? Inasmuch as Freud developed the concept of defense as primarily a defense against affects, he also recognized the centrality of emotions. In contrast to the equal-weight discharge–elimination view of affects, Krystal (1988) introduced the idea that affects—even painful emotional states—are constructive and useful because all affects function as signals. In fact, he sees "the inability to read and integrate one's own feelings as the core of most psychopathology" (Orange, 1995, p. 89) and the ability to tolerate emotional distress and to be able to differentiate, articulate, and desomatize affect as the basic gauge of mental health. He views affect as an originally undifferentiated somatic response that a child, through the help of good-enough emotional responsiveness to his or her feelings, will learn to tolerate and name. Krystal (1988) names the ability to bear the intensity of emotional pain without excessive escapes into anesthetics such as drugs, alcohol, food, or emotional deadness "affect tolerance" (p. 91). The ability to hold and observe our own emotions is thus a fundamental prerequisite to being connected to ourselves and others and to knowing who we are.

By "alexithymic," Krystal (1988) meant those patients who cannot use emotions as signals to themselves. They cannot recognize their own or others' emotions; rather, they have a somatic, undifferentiated, vague, unverbalized emotional life. Instead of recognizing what they feel, they may become numb or physically ill.

CLINICAL VIGNETTE: AFFECTS AND THE RISK OF RELATEDNESS

In my work with one such patient, Mrs. S, it was necessary for me to validate her need to keep all feeling at a very low level of intensity in order to maintain a sense of safety. We needed to interpret not so much what she felt as what it was like for her to experience feeling. Over time, we developed a humorous routine in which I would ask her what she felt. She would respond with a roll of her eyes and say, "You know I don't know, but I could take a cognitive stab at it," and I would respond, "Good, I'm happy to take whatever you offer." In this playful manner, we were able to slowly approach her feeling state. For a long time, it was necessary for me not to make a big deal about what she felt. She had identified and banded together with her extremely emotionally detached, rational, and often absent father in order to survive the collapses and shameful behavior of her alcoholic mother. Her emotional life thus remained unresponded to and undifferentiated or was felt as endangering her task of taking care of her mother. Her constant headaches and nasal infections can probably best be understood as somatization of her feelings of rage and despair. I came to understand my modulation of my own emotional responses as providing a soothing and safe holding environment that would allow her to discover her own feelings. She needed to experience my sense of confidence in her through my ability to wait for her expression of feeling. Krystal (1988) writes that "patients need to become acquainted with their emotions as signals, often unpleasant, but manageable" (p. 29) and that "one must appreciate the subjective experience of patients whose affect tolerance is impaired. They are persons who were traumatized in childhood, whose affects are allowed to flood them," resulting in "a lifelong dread of affects. In such patients, the genetic development of the affects themselves often has suffered, causing the affects to be mostly somatized, poorly verbalized, and poorly differentiated" (p. 29). Interestingly, my patient would correct me if I discussed her lack of feeling: she did have feelings but rarely in my presence. Intersubjectively, I can now reflect that my deep feelings of doubt concerning my chances of ever being able to help her must have been communicated to her. While I recognized her physiological symptoms as difficulties in her affect tolerance, I only much later understood that it was my own amnesia concerning my own early deep feelings of estrangement, my own feelings of "forgotten" pain, that blocked my ability to recognize hers. We can readily understand why Krystal calls the development of affect tolerance "a life-long task" (p. 24). We must "be aware to what extent similar and/or symmetric aspects of our own personalities . . . can be unconsciously activated simply by contact with the patient and work furtively within us like a saboteur, hindering the satisfactory development of dialogue and mutual work" (Momigliano and Robutti, 1992, p. 20). I would expand on this thought and include all aspects of our personalities on a continuum of unconscious to conscious experience that is potentially mutually activated in every encounter. In addition, I would not describe mutuality as only working as a saboteur—even though, as in this case, it often does—but rather as a given within the intersubjective field. "The fact of envisaging the analytic relationship as the meeting of two equally involved people increases the analyst's responsibility" (p. xxvi).

While serving to illustrate several of Krystal's highly valuable insights, this vignette also clarifies a point of difference between his and intersubjectivity theory's views of affective development. While he recognizes the environmental role in the development of affect intolerance, he sees affect regulation primarily as an individual task and mental health as the individual's ability to cope with this task. On the other hand, intersubjectivity theory holds that the "intersubjective field shapes and on the other hand, affect . . . emotional life takes shape as a person's automatic response to a history of parental response to his or her emotional expressions. In adulthood in general, and in treatment in particular, emotional life, shaped by the person's relational history, similarly develops and heals in mutual interchange" (Orange, 1995, p. 92).

ELIMINATING OR EMBRACING THE RISK OF RELATEDNESS?

If we take seriously that patient and therapist form an indissoluble unit and that concerning the human experience of the therapeutic exchange there is no escaping the totality of the mutual influence both partners are subjected to, then we can better understand the impulse to eliminate or mitigate the role of emotions. Infant research has opened our eyes to the fact that there is no unilateral action. Split-second analyses of infant–caretaker interactions demonstrated that the movements and reactions of both partners were like choreographed dyadic dances. In psychotherapy, we can utilize the concept of the spiral movement, "in which every communication is closely linked to the preceding one" (Momigliano and Robutti, 1992, p. 7), as analogous to infant research. In this sense, both partners are completely involved. As we have learned to overcome the myth of the isolated mind, which, to repeat, "bifurcated the subjective world into inner and outer regions, severed both mind from body and cognition from affect, reified and absolutized the resulting divisions, and pictured the mind as an objective entity that takes its place among other objects, a 'thinking thing' that has an inside with contents and that looks out on an external world from which it is essentially estranged" (Stolorow et al., 2002, pp. 1–2), we have come to accept the unbearable embeddedness of being. We live in our patients, and our patients live in us. Having overcome these schisms means that the level of total involvement touches all aspects of human experience. I suspect but have no proof that the minuteness and rapidity of the exchange taking place between human beings is much faster than the eye can see or the mind can register. This would mean it is happening and affecting us at all times. If this is true, then I am not sure I would even like to be able to register all the mutual influence taking place. As can be seen, it is not that I cannot understand those who would like to "discharge" affect and downplay the role of emotion in human existence, but I think the chances are as likely as hearing one hand clapping.

FEELINGS OF DISCONNECTEDNESS IN THE SERVICE OF COHESION

In my work with another patient, Mr. L, an intellectual man in his early 30s, I was quite dumbfounded by his way of expressing himself. He spoke in a beautiful, literate way, as if he were describing a protagonist in a 19th-century novel. However, he was also very cryptic about what he felt. He would speak in what I came to think of as headlines but delivering no text and leaving out any connections between the topics. At times, I felt a little bit crazy listening to him and began to doubt my ability to think, even though I always enjoyed the tender musicality of his thoughts. At first, I reacted like an anxious mother, bombarding him with interpretations and questions up to the point of beginning to feel that I was chasing or even persecuting him. Then I remembered my "chair," the obvious—if you're not seeing what you're seeing, then that's what you're seeing. I didn't understand what was going on until I figured out that's what was going on. In this case, what was happening is that my patient didn't want to be found. Finally, it dawned on me that this was very important for him, in some sense existential for his integrity. So I relaxed and stopped hounding him. There followed a sequence of hours in which he was almost entirely silent. I commented on his way of dealing with his feelings. I said that I thought I understood that for him it was very important that he feel safe and that he needed time to commune with himself. At some point, he asked me if I didn't feel left out. I answered that I thought that was the point. I had in fact felt left out in the many preceding months. I had felt frustrated and had felt surges of irritation, but they would fade as soon as I felt a curiosity, tinged with humor, about not understanding in the least what was going on. That saved me from being intrusive—that and the fact that I felt a great tenderness for his struggle to be himself. So I had a lot of work to do on myself: I had to grapple with my feelings of inefficacy, my feelings of being lost on a lunar landscape. Kohut's example of a patient being driven to psychosis by his mother always hiding behind her bridge cards came to mind. What an improbable connection: psychosis and bridge cards! However, Kohut saw being ignored as a major pathogenic factor. I do not mean to imply that my patient was consciously or unconsciously trying to drive me crazy. On the contrary, I am trying to illustrate that it was my own feelings of early disconnectedness that I had to struggle with. My patient rewarded me handsomely for my struggles. My validation of his right to in essence keep his feelings to himself, to protect himself, and to be whatever way he felt like being led him to comment that he enjoyed not subjugating every feeling to the analytic enterprise. We both had a good laugh about that. One man's golden rule is another man's curse. In addition, he revealed to me that his depressive mother had a way of using him and what he revealed about himself to vitalize herself. He told me that he had been grateful that I hadn't reacted with anger to his silences like his father, who was given to violent, rageful outbursts.

Let us retrace the steps of our dyadic dance. My patient was trying to find out whether I would react like his mother to his need to be delineated. Did I need him to regulate my sense of self-worth, would I rob him of his expansive and proud self-expression, would that be the price of his tie to me? The pride he felt and showed me in his literary ability to describe his life is certainly a talent in its own right, while it also encoded his fear of being exploited or usurped. His silences, his refusal to provide the links in his train of thought, and his silent need to have a safe place to commune with his emotional life were also an expression of his hope to forge a new relationship with an idealized father figure who would not react with rageful one-upmanship but who would instead provide a soothing background tie allowing him to hide or show himself to the degree and in the manner he saw fit.

He traveled back and forth on the transference continuum, between the pole of hopeful and new selfobject needs and the conflictual, defensive pole of fearing a retraumatization according to how open and emotionally available he experienced me. The fact that I did at first react much like his mother and in my silent flights of irritation like his father codetermined the course of our therapeutic dialogue. The intersubjective nature of our encounter is readily visible throughout the course of our work.

This model of how psychoanalysis can be practiced today is, as Momigliano and Robutti (1992) explained, based on the idea that "the patient is the best colleague we are likely to have, not because he is our therapist, but because he helps us to understand him. This turns upside down the old Freudian model (which, as we know, included the use of military and surgical metaphors) according to which the patient comes to analysis absolutely determined to oppose and to present strenuous resistance to the analyst's work, and the old Kleinian one which tended above all to insist on underlining the aggressive and envious aspects of the patient's words and behavior" (p. 20). It is not my intention to polemicize against or oversimplify other psychoanalytic models. Such models have, however, lent themselves to a clinical sensibility that is still to be found today. This attitude views the patient if not as an enemy, then as a trickster, demanding our constant vigilance. A critical, skeptical stance is then mistaken for neutrality.

In Krystal's view, the affect most feared is love, not aggression. Had I seen my patient's actions as based on an inherent aggressive drive, as the sole property of an intrapsychic conflict, and not also as the product of our very intersubjective encounter, I would have been sorely tempted to "discharge" my own helplessness in the guise of righteous anger about the patient's refusal to offer his feelings on the altar of metapsychological truth. If we do not recognize the intersubjective nature—in its depth—of the therapeutic encounter, for instance, as in this example when I was initially unable to deal with my own painful reactions to my patient, that is precisely when we could be misled to silently exclaim, "That's aggressive!" and to attribute our reaction solely to the patient. Spezzano (1993) notes, "To refuse to think about one's affects in the way the analyst thinks about them is not resistance; to refuse to think playfully and imaginatively about one's affects is resistance" (p. 231). To think playfully, however, requires the analyst's abilty to provide and create with the patient a potential, transitional space, a holding environment (Winnicott, 1965), so that the "analytic situation can act as an incubator for affects that are not yet fully developed" and in which "the analyst's principal task is to safeguard the delicate and decisive transitional area between the spoken and the unspoken, the experienced and the thought, the self and the non-self" (Bezoari and Ferro, 1992, p. 59). Kohut (1984) further developed this line of thinking with the concept of the intact self–selfobject tie as providing the cocoon in which experiences of hitherto subjectively dangerous affects can safely reemerge. At a later point, we will come to Socarides and Stolorow's (1984/1985) important contribution on the relationship between selfobject functions and the integration of affect into the organization of self-experience.

Interpretations do not serve the purpose of unmasking the truth about the patient; rather, the accuracy and the therapeutic effect both produce and are the product of the intersubjective bond. Thus, only after I allowed my patient to teach me that he felt that his sense of psychological survival was tied to his refusal to share his feelings, that he feared having them changed and losing them, was I in the position to convey this insight. This, in turn, showed him that I was affectively attuned to him. As a result, we cocreated a safe-enough space in which we could begin to playfully elaborate the complexities of his emotional life. In line with Kohut's (1984) concept of defensiveness, I had to understand that the patient was, in part, practicing a form of defensive self-holding of his affect state until I was able to offer him an analytic holding environment that provided the safety to explore his feelings. Initially, his resistance was not to knowing but to repeating the intrusion of the thinking of the other, the analyst. Potentially, both the analysand and the analyst are threatened by the subversion of their subjectivity in the intersubjective field.

UNDERSTANDING MUTUALITY IN THE THERAPEUTIC PROCESS

Let us look at this intersubjective phenomenon from the perspective of an old psychoanalytic iconoclast and brave innovator, Harald Searles. In his paper "The Patient as the Therapist to His Analyst" (1979), he states a view that can be considered a forerunner of intersubjectivity theory: "Innate among man's most powerful strivings . . . is an essentially therapeutic striving," and "as for the appreciably larger percentage of human beings who become patients in psychoanalysis and psychotherapy I am suggesting here . . . that the patient wants to give therapy to, as well as receive therapy from, his doctor; . . . in transference terms the patient's illness expresses his unconscious attempt to cure the doctor" (p. 380–81). I must admit that I had to laugh out loud when I read these lines. I appreciated the old rebel's taking the wind out of the pompous sails that we make use of to glide over the rough seas of emotional turmoil. It also brought to mind the old therapist's joke concerning our motivation for being therapists: "So what do we do after we cure our mother? Continue, because it's too late to learn anything else." We would, however, have to amend his statement by deuniversalizing it and contextualizing it further.

Obviously, patients come into treatment not to cure their doctors but to alleviate emotional pain. However, inasmuch as their transference is a product of their original intersubjective development and inasmuch as we, as their therapists, lend ourselves to our patients' experiencing us as a repetition or actually repeating aspects of the conflictual, pathogenic, or even traumatogenic emotional experiences of our patients' past, the idea that patients will try to cure us is not as far-fetched as it may first seem. It is our task then to differentiate between patients' attempt to "cure" us through the same means they tried to maintain the ties to their caretakers—that is, for example, through pathological accommodation—and their hope that we will react differently and allow them to have a new object experience. Furthermore, some patients may be trying to unconsciously show us hidden aspects of our personalities that are blocking the unfolding of their emotions. In this sense, our cure is their cure and adds another dimension to their vested interest in our well-being.

The reason I quote Searles is to emphasize how inextricably we are interwoven in the process of cure: not because we seek relief from our patients for our own emotional ills but because they will be called into play to some degree by the mutual exchange with our patients. The extent to which we accept that the interplay of subjectivities is a sine qua non of psychoanalysis, especially at moments of blockage in the process, demands that we must work with and understand, as a matter of course, our own limitations and pathologies. To the experienced practitioner, it is no big secret that we can add the idea of the completely analyzed, healthy analyst to our list of psychoanalytic myths. We do need to explore further how the risk of relatedness upholds such myths.

CLINICAL EXAMPLE OF MUTUAL REGULATION IN A SEXUALIZED TRANSFERENCE

I think I can best illustrate this with a clinical example. When I was a young analyst in New York, still in training, I accepted into treatment a woman, Mrs. A, in her late 20s. During our first encounter, I was immediately deeply touched by the pain of her existence and her fragility. At the same time, I remember being irritated by what I experienced as an impervious, demanding neediness. I felt she had a cold haughtiness that distressed me, as much as I leaped inwardly to the task of her rescue. My experience of her as arrogant, as I later came to understand, was a psychological form of self-defense against critical inner voices and an attempt to stay on top, lest she wind up on the bottom. It was, in other words, an expression of a defensive grandiosity, compensating and overriding painful inner states of annihilation.

Her mother was a cold and controlling person for whom the patient could do nothing right. "You're useless," her mother endlessly told her. Her father was attentive but seductive toward his daughter and would take her on hunting trips, during which the two of them would stay at small hotels, the father displaying his daughter at lunches and dinners as if she were his girlfriend. There was never any actual, physical sexual abuse, but the atmosphere was ripe with incestuous longings.

She was married to a man who lacked tenderness and who was sexually brutally demanding, not totally devoid of devotion but in the manner of a pasha bestowing favors, expecting rich rewards. She attempted to free herself from her low sense of self-esteem and the oppression of her husband by trying to find a job that would give her financial independence. She suffered from the slights of her coworkers and let herself be exploited by her bosses. Her sense of outrage matched the extent of a frightening, crumbling sense of self-experience.

As treatment progressed, she became increasingly suicidal as a reaction to her dependency needs. She feared being usurped and controlled by me and, on a deeper level, to face her feelings of nonexistence, to be seen as useless and rejected by me should she allow herself to show me the extent of her need to be a little girl and her hope to be finally cherished and protected by a mother figure. Fearing a repeat of the devastating rejection in the mother transference, she warded off these feelings by being unconsciously seductive toward me. She would describe her sexual encounters with her husband in detail, emphasizing the size of his penis but also the pain that it sometimes caused her. At the same time, she was teasingly seductive in the way that she looked at me and her physical comportment. Clearly, this was a repeat of her relationships with her parents. She turned to the father/analyst in a seductive manner in order to secure some amount of attention while avoiding her deeper feelings of annihilation.

I, in turn, responded on both levels and was distressed on both levels. Primarily, I felt afraid that she would concretize her feelings of annihilation by taking her own life. She did, in fact, attempt suicide with pills at one point. My own mother transference was triggered here in my feelings that I must save her and in my conviction that I was inadequate and unable to do so. My mother had also been partly coldly removed, belittling, and seductive. Therefore, my past intersubjective field was an inverse mirror of both aspects of her transference, collapsing both the rejection of her mother and the seductivenes of her father into my own mother transference.

While I was aware of being mesmerized and enmeshed by her subtle and not-so-subtle erotic overtures, I felt helpless and worried by my erotic feelings toward my patient. I felt that my awareness of my response safeguarded me and allowed me to continue working through this embroiled analytic field, giving me enough decentered distance to function analytically. An incident at the end of one session taught me one of my first—but certainly not last—lessons about the power of the unconscious and, more germane to the theme of this book, the depth of involvement in analytic relationships and the truly scary risks of relatedness. She had ended the session in despair, saying that her life was at a dead end, that the analysis and I were useless. Getting up from the couch, my patient reached for a cigarette in her purse, turned to me (I was still sitting), and, seemingly out of the blue, said, "Are you going to fuck me now, or can I go smoke this cigarette?" I was so dumbstruck that I responded with nervous laughter and, mumbling something unintelligible, hastily accompanied her to the door. While I hadn't thought that my tongue had been hanging to the floor, apparently my patient responded to something I had transmitted that I hadn't been aware of, at least at that moment.

Both my supervisor and my training analyst came to the rescue. My supervisor, after I had reported this session, said that my patient's sexuality was actually more akin to a nosebleed, thus firmly placing her on the level of "hysteric" behavior. My analyst deepened my understanding of the session by giving me a more intersubjective perspective. He pointed out that while my patient was being seductive—in the repetitive, conflictual, defensive dimension of the transference—she actually was hoping—in the selfobject dimension of the transference—that I would respond to her need to not be seduced. She was hoping that I would offer her a new object experience, a feeling of being cherished in her totality as a human being, and not only for a part of her, that is, her sexuality, which she felt was a prerequisite for securing my affections, in other words, that I would recognize the oedipal transference as a defense against the preoedipal transference.

In terms of working through my own issues, I had to understand that the desperateness of my anxious need to save my patient was fueled by my own past need to rescue my mother from her lifelong depression and by my own feelings of annihilation and rejection, feelings of annihilation that I had been, much like my patient, warding off with the vitalizing effect of my eroticized responsiveness to her. It wasn't so much that I wished to penetrate her as that I longed to penetrate the foggy depths of her feelings of nothingness in order to contact a place where she felt alive and that would enliven me. Analogously, it was Kohut (1984) who made the point about a patient who as a young boy felt driven to see a girl's genitals as a concretization of his need to see a response in his rejecting mother's face, a return to a more archaic, psychosomatic experience, in lieu of a lack of a symbolic response. For both of us, the eroticized component of our feelings was a breakdown product of a threatened sense of self-experience, of a drivenness in the service of a cohesion-maintaining function, and not of a drive directed at a separately experienced object seeking release.

From the view of intersubjectivity theory, we can see how the therapeutic process was a product of both the subjectivities involved. On a fundamental level, my anxiety about being able to help my patient was probably organized by her as a lack of confidence that she was capable of being healed. Thus, "when we are better able to bear our own anxiety and the inevitable sense of impotence when faced with what we really can't mend, then we are also able to convey to the patient the possibility of tolerating [her] sense of death and the horror of what [she] is feeling" (Momigliano and Robutti, 1992, pp. 16–17). In addition, "If it is true that with each patient the analyst experiences a new countertransference micropathology (Baranger and Baranger, 1961/1962), a successful analysis will have transformative and liberating effects not only on the patient, but on the analyst, too. As A. and F. Meotti (1988) say, "every analysis that is successfully, if imperfectly, terminated, is also the successful analysis of a part of ourselves as yet unknown to us" (Bezoari and Ferro, 1992, p. 64). While the unknown need not be frightening per se, Bion's (1990) comment on the two frightenend people in treatment also points to the possible risks involved as we face our "micropathologies."

Working with patients, there will always be different degrees of entanglement and involvement, and the work will be more or less difficult and successful, depending on which issues are triggered in the analyst and depending on the extent of the problems these issues present to the analyst. This, in turn, will determine the "emotional availability" (Orange, 1995) that we can offer our patients. So, while I think I would have reacted to and treated this patient differently today, I will always have blind spots, the nature of which I can discover only after I have gone—or suffered—through them. Different patients will touch us in different ways, some in the dramatic fashion described previously, some even by a seeming absence of intense feelings, but in each instance we will find ourselves somewhere on the keyboard of emotions, and we will always be played, even if we've never heard the music before. We can't expect to be able to work through what happens in the intersubjective field in effigy, that is, by treating it as if it were due merely to someone else's fantasy.

I think we can now explain the past psychoanalytic bias "to describe and work with emotion as if it were a cognition or an instinctual derivative," something to be gotten rid of (Orange, 1995, p. 97), and the cognitive tilt that sees insight as the main curative factor. If we understand, as Ferenczi did, "that psychoanalysis is emotional medicine for emotional ills" (p. 98), then we can better understand our own resistance to enter into the complexity and depth of the emotional relationships we are required to have with our patients if we hope to help them. Psychoanalysis is not a detective story that we can safely regard from the outside, trying to detect who did what to whom and why. Rather, to understand a patient, we have to become part of his or her emotional story and let them become part of ours. On the level of intense, partly quite painful emotional experiencing that is needed to work effectively, we can't hide behind professional circumferences but are exposed to all the dangers inherent in living.

THE SENSE OF THINGS: THE COMPLEXITY OF EMOTIONAL LIFE

This section on the complexity of emotional life is indebted to the seminal work of Donna Orange, in particular her book *Emotional Understanding: Studies in Psychoanalytic Epistemology* (1995). Her view of the complexity of emotions has great value for our clinical sensibility and can offer us a tremendous sense of relief in the difficult task of understanding the vast universe of the inner lives of our patients. Her plea against oversimplifying the nature of emotions, to reject an atomistic conception of affects as "a too-easy substitute for instinctual drives as the explanatory foundation in psychoanalysis, with an attentiveness to the totality and complexity of a person's emotional life" (p. 104), is closely related to my theme of the risk of relatedness.

Her description of the three essential features of emotional life sheds much light on why it is emotionally difficult to relate to our patients. She describes it as an unavoidably complex process because all psychic events serve many purposes—as is well known and has been conceptualized in the principle of multiple function (Waelder, 1936)—and have many causes—as conceptualized in the principle of overdetermination (S. Freud, 1910). In our attempts to make order out of chaos, that is, to not be overwhelmed by the immensity of the task to grasp how it feels to be another person, we may "abstract and extract what is inextricable," thus violating "the integrity of a person's experience" (Orange, 1995, p. 96). Often when patients disagree with us and point out the incompleteness of our understanding, this is not because of resistance—except a healthy resistance to being misunderstood. Rather, it underscores the complexity of any emotional life. For instance, my patient who was keeping himself hidden from me commented, after hearing the vignette, that it wasn't only that he needed to protect his integrity but also that he feared my disinterest concerning his inner life in a profound way. Oversimplifying an emotion of a patient serves a self-holding purpose of the therapist, as we try to hold on to our sense of things while understanding the other. An atomistic view of affect serves as a bulwark against our own fears of feeling like the blind leading the blind. Thus, a deep comprehension of the complexity of emotions can help us while we stumble along in the darkness. Whenever I offer an interpretation, I try to remember to listen very closely to the tone of my patient's voice. Often she may agree verbally, but the cadence of the answer reveals that, as Winnicott is reported as having once remarked, my interpretation served only to reveal to the patient how far off the mark I was. Interesting for me, then, is to note how much discipline I have to exert, not to have my need to be right interfere with my understanding my patient. As I explain to my supervisees, in an attempt to internalize my own clinical approach, because I understand their nervousness about the task at hand all too well, we can shed the weight of immaculate perception if we can accept the complexity of emotional life. Relax, I want to shout, the darkness is just beginning.

THE RELATIONAL CHARACTER OF EMOTIONAL LIFE

"A second essential feature of emotional life is its relational character" (Orange, 1995, p. 97). Di Chiara (in Momigliano and Robutti, 1992), citing Rykoff, asks, "Why is it that in psychoanalysis the affects and their inter-relations are disregarded? . . . The analyst should realize that the patient, when speaking about himself, is trying to set up a relationship with the analyst" (p. 25). Orange (1995), in contrast to Krystal, does not see emotion as mere internal signal. Instead, the relational theory of human nature in psychoanalysis conceptualizes emotion contextually. "Emotions are responses to relational events or needs, and emotional expression is an attempt to connect, or to regulate connection, with another. . . . Emotional experience begins, continues, and heals in specific intersubjective contexts" (p. 97). Clinically, this is a very important point to fathom because whenever we may be tempted to distance ourselves from our patients' emotions by thinking that their feeling is "inappropriate," we've forgotten the context and the question, Inappropriate for whom and to which situation? If instead, as in intersubjectivity theory, we see emotions as formed by past intersubjective fields and evoked or triggered by the present intersubjective field, then we are automatically implicated in any "inappropriateness." On first impression, my patient's question about whether I wanted to have sex with her certainly struck me as highly "inappropriate" and left me scrambling for my analytic high horse.

If it seems that I am endlesssly singing the song of the indissoluble unit and beating the drum of contextuality, or of a reifed fusion, if one may get the wrong impression that I ignore the need for self-distinctness and demarcation and self boundaries—but even these are won or lost only in relational contexts—then it is because it is so hard to overcome the Cartesian mind. I must sing loudly so that I can hear myself. I am also aware of how my own history and subjectivity dovetail with the theory that I uphold. The idea that we are isolated beings cut off from all that sustains us is so deeply ingrained as to warrant "loud" protest. In treatment, it means that we are always to some degree involved in our patients' feelings. That is, indeed, almost unbearable and the reason we say that understanding is endured. In our view, emotion does not reside solely in the individual.

THE EMOTIONALITY OF EMOTIONAL LIFE

The third feature is not only that emotions are complex and relational but also that "emotional life is emotional" (Orange, 1995, p. 97). Orange sees emotion as "primarily noncognitive and nonverbal relational response" (p. 97) linked with cognition or schemata but having its own reality. Orange takes issue with the cognitive cast of psychoanalytic language with the talk of "organizing principles" (Stolorow et al., 1987), representation, and schemata, because this mitigates and marginalizes the emotionality of emotions and their centrality in psychoanalysis. She prefers to speak of "emotional organizing principles" and "emotional modes of inference," pointing out that "because these are emotional, they usually operate in such an automatic manner that identifying them is difficult" (Orange, 1995, pp. 97–98).

Now we can better understand Mitchell's (1993) emphasis on the value of confusion and ambiguity, "the need to suspend judgment, premature understanding, and forced clarity" (p. 32). In trying to relate to and understand our emotional lives, we are diving into dark waters and fishing in deep seas.

EMOTIONAL MEMORY

Orange's (1995) concept of emotional memory gives a new perspective to what we are trying to make sense of in psychoanalysis, adding an important component to explaining psychoanalytic understanding. At the same time, it illuminates why we may have such difficulties in understanding our patients and ourselves. She argues that "most experiencing is visceral, emotional and only partly organized" (p. 106). It consists of the largely noncognitive, nonverbal, visceral knowledge we have of ourselves and is based on how our past experiences have encoded themselves into our whole being as memory. Intersubjectivity theory sees all psychic events as a product of the interplay between differently organized subjectivities, and therefore memory also can be understood only as relational. Loewald (1960) also sees memory as inherently relational; patients don't have a past, they are their past. Bollas (1989) has explained that, as infants, we internalize "the mother's actual idiom of care, which is a complex network of rules for being and relating" (p. 195). The child organizes the rules and assumptions of the interactions with his caretakers into a deep personal structure. Therefore, the moods we have, the way we treat ourselves as adults, is a form of remembering how we were treated as children. Emotional memory, Orange (1995) further points out, is neither necessarily pathological nor pathogenic, nor is it the same as unconsciousness.

CLINICAL EXAMPLE OF EMOTIONAL MEMORY

A brief clinical example will help illustrate how emotional memory works. A patient, Mrs. N, lay silently on the couch at the beginning of a session, covering her eyes with her hands. She sometimes has difficulties ordering her thoughts because they seem to charge through her mind like a herd of stampeding animals, kicking up mental dust, and wreaking emotional havoc. For the same reason, she finds it hard to find an entrée into the session. We have come to the conclusion that it is helpful to her for me to somehow start the ball rolling. This gives her the necessary sense of a containing structure, much like the covering of her face. On this day, I began by commenting that she looked quite morose. She answered by describing what keeps her from sleep. Ugly thoughts come up of feeling rejected, and small incidents of feeling slighted during the day haunt her. Underlying these thoughts is a pervasive, basic sense of loneliness. She can fall asleep only by reading until she drifts off. Reading also banishes the painful feelings. She remembered having difficulties sleeping throughout her life. Only if she can distract herself or if someone close lies next to her does sleep come. Then she feels held. Worse than the feeling of loneliness is what she feels when she wakes up in the middle of the night. "My body is floating out there, somewhere in the universe, without oxygen. Way off in the distance, I see tiny points of light. I feel completely paralyzed then." This comes very close to Kohut's (1984) example of the devastating meaning of being entirely cut off from a selfobject milieu. He told the story of the astronauts who thought their damaged capsule could not return to earth. Asked if they preferred to endlessly remain in orbit after their demise, they preferred to reenter the earth's atmosphere, even if it meant being burned to death. Being endlessly cut off from their home was more horrible than some kind of reconnection, even if it also cost them their lives.

She was told by her family that she couldn't sleep as a baby and that she had been a "screamer," causing her mother distress. Her grandmother took charge by sending the overwrought mother off on a 4-week holiday to "recuperate" and by locking her in a dark bathroom, letting her scream until she finally "gave up" and fell silent. She said that she "remembered this emotionally, feeling abandoned, lonely and locked away." I felt shocked by the brutality of this kind of child rearing. The patient remembered the painful states but could not put it into a relational context. On the contrary, she felt that she was to blame for being such a difficult child. Only when I functioned in the role of witness to what I felt was a traumatogenic part of her history, linking her vague but all-encompassing feelings of loss to the fact that she was left by her mother and exposed to a brutal lack of emotional attunement by the grandmother, could she begin to understand what her emotional memory had encoded. She had internalized the rules and regulations, the idiom of care, into a part of her personality, for which she blamed only herself. We could begin to comprehend why she has difficulties holding her feelings and making sense of them. The lack of attunement to her inner life left her at the mercy of chaotic feelings. We could also better comprehend why she needed to feel my interest in the concretized form of making the first contact with her rather than remaining caught in the endless orbit of her own silent sense of being cut off, floating on the couch. Then she felt safe and held enough to sort out what had before been an incomprehensible dark mood.

Her mother had not been able to handle her daughter's painful affects—the grandmother had treated the mother much in the same way—instead asking her to face life with a stiff upper lip. To deal with her sense of rejection and to restore a sense of inner balance, my patient developed a form of pride in the fact that she could deal with life on her own; asking someone for help engendered a feeling of shame, much the same way she had been shamed when she asked her mother for comfort.

Thus, she encoded these experiences by developing an emotional organizing principle that became a central building block of her personality, demanding that she be autonomous. The emotional memory of loneliness and rejection was a felt threat to her psychological homeostasis and came to haunt her when she tried to sleep because falling asleep meant letting go, being dropped into an abyss, with no one to catch her. Falling asleep and, even more so, awakening alone in the depths of the night is then a repeat of the total loss of a selfobject milieu, something like a dark bathroom, something like a small death.

If emotional memory is the result of our encoding of our relational history, of which only a small part has been cognitively processed, then it is important for us to learn that what we are able to say about ourselves is not equivalent to what we know about ourselves. This is significant clinically, as it explains why insight, even in the sense of emotional understanding alone, is not curative. It does not erase our emotional history. "We need not feel that psychoanalysis fails because insight does not remove emotional memory. We cannot expect that it should" (Orange, 1995, p. 120). Again, this explains why our patients so often may say, "So now that I know that, what does it change?" They are right inasmuch as emotional memory goes beyond the realm of words and beyond our ability to capture our experiences in words. However, understanding the impact of what goes on beyond words helps us as clinicians reassess the extent of what we can understand—namely, often, not all that much—and to reevaluate the difficulty in comprehending the histories that our patients are. It expresses respect for "that part of the psyche that lives in the wordless world" (Bollas, 1987, p. 3, cited in Orange, 1995, p. 111). Mitchell (1993) makes an interesting and, to my mind, amusing comment about this point that I feel is valid nonetheless. He writes, "In a reversal of traditional psychoanalytic machismo, it now sometimes appears that the capacity to contain the dread of not knowing is a measure of analytic virtue; the fewer convictions, the better and the braver!" (p. 43).

EMOTIONAL MEMORY AND INTERPRETATION IN THE INTERSUBJECTIVE MATRIX

While the timing of interpretations is still important, we can now also base that timing on our tacit knowledge of our patients and ourselves and thus debunk the myth of the perfectly lanced interpretation and view them more in terms of trial balloons that we send aloft. We can better accept our limitations and become more playfully experimental, accepting the possibility of making many mistakes. We can deemphasize the bias of the negative that understandably comes with the territory of pain that we so often deal with but that has made us forget that life is not only tears but also laughter. The severity with which patients often judge themselves is lightened if they can see that we also make mistakes and are willing to stumble about without self-recrimination.

We also know that it really isn't only the understanding of our patients that helps them but more what the effect is of arriving at that understanding together with them. Stolorow et al. (1987) have pointed out that the mutative impact of our interpretations lies in the insights conveyed because these interpretations demonstrate the extent of our emotional attunement to our patient's emotional states and developmental needs. "The analyst's interpretations are not disemboodied transmissions of insight about the analytic relationship. They are an inherent, inseparable component of that very bond, and their therapeutic action derives from the intersubjective matrix in which they crystallize" (p. 101). It helps us to remember that it is our patients who are the experts on knowing what it feels like to be them, and in that regard we are the pupils sitting in the first row, willing to learn. "This more modest attitude can produce a 'let's figure it out together' replacement for the psychoanalytic emphases on verbal interpretation as something an analyst gives to a patient and on the analyst's authority or expertise" (Orange, 1995, p. 124). This concept of emotional memory thus upgrades the value of tacit knowledge, implicitly cautioning us to verbally leave well enough alone at times and to trust the healing power of the emotional bond.

We can watch our patients working on and being worked on by the constancy of our presence, simultaneously attracted and repelled by the possibilities. Much of what transpires in therapy is never subjected to an explanation. When asking patients at the end of treatment what helped them, they will often say it was the reliability of our attentiveness, or they will pick out some incident of feeling touched by our contact, usually expressly not in a "therapeutic way." Not so frequently, they will mention the changes they have undergone in comparison to how they once were. As their therapist, I might cite the nodal points of their therapeutic process, but it doesn't seem to evoke all that much interest or emotional response, leading me to believe that what has been encoded and formed new emotional memory reflects the feeling of having been attended to, which, in turn, forms the basis of a new sense of safety and comfort with being who they are and living in a welcoming world. In general, the lack of interest may reflect that whatever happened has already been encoded in a new emotional memory and therefore does not at this point require a replay on the level of verbal consciousness.

EMOTIONAL AVAILABILITY

Emotional availability, a term introduced and elaborated by Orange (1995), is, in my view, another central concept for our understanding of the role of affects in treatment and is crucial for our clinical sensibility. The shift to a relational emphasis in psychoanalysis, she explains to us, has led us to think less about the success or failure of analysis in terms of the patient's pathology and more in terms of the fit between patient and analyst. Thus, the emotional availability of a therapist for a particular patient has moved into the foreground of understanding how and why a therapeutic relationship may or may not work. She defines emotional availability as "an active and responsive preparedness for empathic understanding" (p. 125). It is not a certain type of intervention, interpretation, or response. Instead, it is nonspecific, taking on many forms, often nonverbal. "Like sensitive parents, we must be ready to adjust our mode of emotional availability to suit the receptive capacities of a particular patient" (p. 126).

The issue here, as so often when faced with patients' needs, is not oral "greed" or aggressive needs for dominance, nor is it patients' envy for what they may feel we have and they don't. Even if so, it is often related to a felt sense of deprivation or insecurity concerning their needs. For instance, one patient tested my emotional availability by regularly commenting on the temperature of the room at the beginning of sessions. Sometimes it was too warm, other times too cool, too stuffy, too airy. While a certain edge of hostility or a desire for control did not escape me, I felt on a deeper level that she needed to know whether I would adjust to her specific needs.[5] At a later point, we were able to discuss how her disbelief in anyone being responsive to her necessitated an aggressive undertone and how that then became a self-fulfilling prophecy. We may, as a result of feeling egged on to respond in a certain way, feel tempted to enter into a contest of wills with our patients. While there are certainly inner boundaries that we must be attentive to in ourselves and that may necessitate clarification, this shouldn't keep us from exploring the underlying issues for the patient. More often than not, we are dealing with our patients' uncertainty about their ability to express a feeling or need, which then becomes concretized in statements about such things as room temperature.

"Embracing the concept of emotional availability erases neutrality and anonymity as rules for analytic conduct" (Orange, 1995, p. 127). More precisely, we "adjust how much we reveal to the needs of the individual patient, in the same way that parents attune their level of accessibility to the child" (p. 127). Orange cites the work of the attachment theorists Emde and Sorce (1983), who point out the role of the caretaker's emotional availability for the development of the infant. They claim that the awareness of the child's emotional states and the ability to respond empathically by offering her own emotional expressions as information when the infant is uncertain and looks to her is crucial for infant development. It enhances the infant's curiosity, playfulness, explorativeness, and interest in learning and leads to less clingy behavior. It is not so much that a direct comparison between infants and patients is being drawn or that we are stressing only developmental deficits. However, an analogy holds, in my view, in the face of how fragile we are. Orange's point is that our emotional availability analogously provides the necessary safety that allows exploration and curiosity to unfold in our patients. To create an atmosphere of safety, we need to communicate by our behavior that we are tracking our patients' emotional expressions. In therapy, this occurs in many ways: the tone of our voices (this cannot be overemphasized), the choice of what kind of language we use, and the sounds and faces we make. If the emotional backup is missing, no accuracy of empathy will do. Patients will register the discrepancy, consciously or unconsciously. Again, I hasten to add that this in no way implies that we always make the grade. Emotional availability is hard work, much the same as good-enough parenting, as Orange points out. As such, it has relevance for the theme of this book.

Orange also makes the comparison to Winnicott's (1965) holding environment. The attuned, nonintrusive presence creates the necessary safety for the patient to unfold and articulate his or her own way of being at any given time. For instance, I have a patient in her mid-30s, Mrs. B, who enacts her need for safety by alternately sitting or lying on the couch within one session and by piling the pillows in front of her if she feels unsafe or in need of self-holding or by embracing a pillow as a transitional object. This has been very helpful for me in monitoring her emotional states and her reactions to me. For this patient, who has a history of severe sexual and violent abuse and who has great difficulties in protecting herself from experiences of invasiveness, this noninsistence on a rigid analytic setting has greatly facilitated her experimentation with boundaries and her emotional self-expression. Parenthetically, for other patients, flexibility may mean a strict adherence to the agreed-on setting. For Mrs. B, holding a pillow allowed her to hold on to herself while symbolically holding on to me. Her wish to be held is only surfacing now, after 5 years of treatment, but it still evokes many panicky feelings in terms of both allowing her inner longings to reawaken and her fears of retraumatization by others.

For a very long while, I made no verbal reference to her actions, understanding her need to concretely experiment and solidify various forms of self-articulation and to experience a sense of safety, or holding environment, a feeling that she could rely on my nonintrusive, attuned presence. In this instance, my nonintrusiveness included not making a symbolic interpretation on the basis of my psychological understanding of her developmental state and need. Only after this was firmly established has it become possible to delicately approach a symbolic understanding of her changing emotional needs and the role I play in the shifting intersubjective field. In the case of severe trauma, such as this patient experienced, it will take much time, perhaps up to another 5 years, in order to fully explore the intimacies of mutual exchange as they arise and find expression in this particular intersubjective field. As she has put it, the relational field is "full of sand-holes and land-mines." Sending up trial-balloon interpretations about our relationship still evokes a puzzled response. To think about the effect she may have on me does not occur to her yet. This doesn't keep me from alluding to various aspects of our relatedness in order to, in dynamic systems theory thinking, jar the system once in a while and, by her response and my own, to see where we are. However, I think this vignette clearly demonstrates the primacy of safety and the role that emotional availability plays in terms of what either is or is not done in establishing a facilitating environment.

The "readiness to offer our emotional expressions—verbal, semi-verbal, or non-verbal—is a crucial component of the conversation that creates psychoanalytic understanding" (Orange, 1995, p. 128). We offer our emotional expressions—as a form of emotional availability—as a way of encouraging patients to overcome their insecurities in finding their own emotional expresssion. The purpose is not to do it for the patient but to serve as a "pump-priming" (p. 128). Our willingness to experiment, to not be fearfully tight-lipped or overly elegant, encourages the patient to experiment with her emotional expressions.

CLINICAL EXAMPLE OF EMOTIONAL AVAILABILITY

One man I treated in his early 40s, Mr. O, was extremely inhibited about the way he expressed his feelings. He worked in social services and was guided by his ideals of political justice. His keen sense of social injustice was due partly to his experiences of his father as a tyrannical figure and his identification with his suffering, submissive mother. The expression of his emotions was tightly controlled by an oppressive subjugation to political correctness. Especially in his attempts to be intimate with women, he felt that he had no right to make his needs clear—even when the woman was waving with a signpost. To express a desire, especially as a man, was to be tyrannical like his father and a possible repeat of the injustices his mother had suffered at the hands of his father. In addition, on an even deeper level, it would have threatened the tie to the mother and be experienced as an act of disloyalty. Thus, while I certainly interpreted all these dynamics, I also found myself using a less pristine, more direct way of expressing feelings. While avoiding any demeaning connotations of coarse language, I did make use of venacular expressions in terms of paraphrasing his squeaky-clean formulations of desire toward women. If he said something such as that he would like to get closer to a woman whom he greatly admired, whom he felt was very attractive, and with whom he'd spent the entire night talking in spite of her clear signals that she was also interested in physical intimacy and his obvious interest, I would perhaps say, "I understand, you had the hots for her." This allowed him to be freer in his emotional expressions and the exploration of his feelings. Implicitly, he could identify with being a man, as we were able to share a male perspective concerning the attractiveness of women that didn't imply a negative attitude.

EMOTIONAL AVAILABILITY: OBSTACLES AND LIMITATIONS

Orange (1995) explores several sources of why we might feel reluctant to use the full range of our emotional expressiveness in our attempts to get closer to patients and facilitate their emotional expressiveness. We may be repeating the deprivation experiences in our own analyses with silent and invisible analysts, we may cling to an inflexible, traditional analytic setup and procedures in order to avoid emotional engagement, or we may feel "unanalytic" if we take the risks of being more emotionally expressive. We may also fear being intrusive, in particular, if intrusiveness was an issue in our own childhood. With the man described previously, I felt all these fears. It has taken me nearly 20 years to shake myself free of the traditional analytic persona and to disentangle a restricted use of the idiosyncrasies of my personality from the immense discipline that our profession demands of us. Of course, my greater sense of freedom also has to do with the length of time that I have been practicing, much like a musician, who can improvise only because of having played for many years.

The practice of therapy could also be compared to dancing, a dance in which we struggle—through the free use of our emotions—for a sense of liveliness. Together we swirl and dip, freeze, stamp our feet, defy crazy sorrow, and fall into meditations of the pain to be someone. No matter what we may see in the face of despair, it's always the heart looking for resonance. For therapists, it's important sometimes to free themselves from the fog of pain. As it does make up a large part of our daily fare, it can be equally healing to find a way, together with the patient, to gut-felt laughter, in other words, to use whatever idiosyncratic expression of our emotionality that through our contact reflects that there's still something alive out here!

We may also fear that patients may become too dependent on us and that we could interfere with their idiosyncratic sense of self as a result of offering our own emotional expressions (Orange, 1995). Patients who were never allowed to experience a healthy sense of dependency may respond with very regressive needs. We may panic in face of the immense neediness, feeling that we bit off much more than we can chew. Some patients may develop transferences in which very early stages of developmental arrest are allowed to resume their growth. One such patient, Mrs. B (the patient with a severe history of multiple trauma mentioned earlier) needed to completely withdraw from all adult demands, especially those that pertained to achievement and the pursuit of her career. She also needed to withdraw from many of her former relationships in which her self-worth was closely intertwined with her ability to serve other people's needs. This led to a 2-year period of social disengagement. However, what could be judged from the outside as a disturbing development leading to isolation and an existential threat to her ability to ever be able to resume her working life was in fact an absolutely necessary prerequisite to her being able to develop her own sense of selfhood. In fact, a former colleague pointed out to her that in their professsion a 2-year hiatus meant professional death. At the same time, various doctors and colleagues also warned me that she was close to the point of no return. It required much courage on her part to allow herself to go into a kind of psychological incubator in which the worst damage she suffered could be healed and new ways could be developed. Both of us were sometimes frightened that she wouldn't survive as her basic feeling of being "human junk" was allowed to resurface within the safety of the therapeutic relationship. Often it was my task to hold the lantern high as we traversed the darkest nights of her self-hatred. On other occasions, when I faltered, it was she who would remind me of how far we had come, who would remind me of her belief in my belief in her. Being emotionally available means revisiting our own pain as we inevitably go into resonance with our patients. "Affects," Mitchell (1993) writes, "often work . . . like tuning forks of the same pitch; vibration in one sets off resonance in the others" (p. 61). This may be, as Orange points out another source of wanting to avoid being emotionally available. Sometimes, when a training candidate's suffering may seem more than he or she can bear, I might point out that this will enable him or her to connect to the suffering of their patients. However, no one is ever safe from the risks of relatedness, as the price of an open heart is always potentially to be wounded. Only knowing the dreadfully deadening consequences of living with a heart of stone can give us the courage to remain emotionally available.

Orange (1995) offers a cautionary comment about emotional availability. It does not mean providing patients with whatever they want. It is necessary to "set limits based on the needs of our patients and our own" (p. 132). Kohut's warning to his patient to not be a fool and put his life in danger by reckless driving is a good example. As for therapists, we need to have a wide-awake awareness of how much we can offer. This includes the work with individual patients as well as the amount of work we do. Frieda Fromm-Reichmann was one of the first therapists, to my knowledge, who admonished us to take extremely good care of ourselves, for instance, by having as rich a life outside our work as possible. In general, it appears to me that this seems less easy for therapists to accomplish than it should be, but it can be easily explained by at least one reason, namely, that many of us came to this work as a result of having had various caretaker roles in our original families and thus being acccustomed to standing back in the face of other people's needs. Knowing how and what we can offer also must be based on an ongoing comprehension of our limitations. "Emotional availability is always limited by the particularity of analyst and patient" (p. 133). Our emotional history will govern our cotransference and set limits to our emotional availability. However, like any other human experience, it will rise and fall, expand and contract, within the fluidity of any given relational field. "Psychoanalysis is a process involving, most fundamentally, the hopes and dreads of its two participants" (Mitchell, 1993, p. 9).

THE ROLE OF AFFECTIVITY IN THE ORGANIZATION OF SELF-EXPERIENCE

We come now to Socarides and Stolorow's (in Stolorow et al., 1987) contribution alluded to earlier on the role of selfobject functions and the integration of affect into the organization of self-experience. They point out that for many analytic investigators and infant researchers, affects are pivotol for the organization of self-experience. For Stern (1985), affectivity is a "self-invariant," contributing to the development of "the sense of a core self" (p. 69, cited in Stolorow et al., 1987, p. 67). "Interaffectivity," or the sharing of mutual affective states, is the most clinically important feature of intersubjective relatedness, determining for the infant "the shape of and extent of the shareable inner universe" (p. 152, cited in Stolorow et al., 1987, p. 67). For Demos (1987), it is the recurrent affect states around which the infant's sense of self becomes crystallized. She also points out the critical role of affect responsiveness in allowing the infant to develop its own affect- and self-regulatory capacities. For all these authors, affect integration and the intersubjective matrix in which it occurs is central for the development and consolidation of self-experience. When affects are met with "the requisite affirming, accepting, differentiating, synthesizing and containing responses from caregivers" (Stolorow et al., 1987, p. 67), they can become integrated and function as organizers of self-experience. In the face of a constant lack of affective attunement, affective reactions will be dissociated or disavowed either because they threaten the fragile structuralizations that have been achieved or because the child senses that they would endanger the tie to the caregiver. Having feelings at all must then be defended against, as they are felt to be a threat. Thus, these minute but significant derailments of affect integration lead to a basic sense of vulnerability and a propensity to self-fragmentation. The accumulated effect of this separation from one's feelings will be a weakened sense of selfhood and a disbelief in the sustaining experience of the other. Disconnecting from feelings is like losing bits of selfhood in the service of maintaining the tie to the other or maintaining an intrapsychic status quo. As Mrs. N, the patient with the sleeping difficulties and the sense of bereft abandonment, put it succinctly, "Every child immediately knows what the parents need and does it, no questions asked. That's how you survive." Basch (1985, cited in in Stolorow et al., 1987) also notes how the early lack of affect attunement leads to a general doubt in the ability to share emotional states, creating a sense of isolation and shame in regard to one's own needs. I would add that it can also lead to a sense of existential shame, a feeling that one doesn't really have the right to exist. Both S. Freud (1915b) and Basch (1985) believed that, in treatment, defense is always against affect. Mrs. N also mentioned that in looking at family videos, she seemed to barely be present in a frame for any length of time; instead, she was always just passing through the picture "or tucked away in a corner like a ghost. It occurred to me, why am I never really in the picture? That's what I've always felt like, a ghost." Later in treatment, when we were discussing her deep sense of loneliness and her frustration about not being able to say to a friend, "Come over, I need you," she commented how profoundly such a question would embarrass her. To ask was simply "unthinkable." She said she would need "at least five invitations" in order to even contemplate expressing such a need. As we explored this issue, it became clear not only that she needed such an amount of reassurance in order to begin to feel welcome but also that a great sense of sorrow arose when she allowed herself to contemplate these reactions. Thus, we could clarify how stating a need was dangerous for her sense of inner stability, as she feared being overwhelmed by an instant recall of a lifetime of rejection, therefore threatening the brittle sense of autonomy she had been forced to create and hold on to. Furthermore, she feared being ridiculed for her neediness as well as her lack of ability to "autonomously" organize what she needed. Her friends complained about her being oversensitive and demanded that she be able to "speak up" about her needs, thus reconfirming her mother's "idiom of care," which demanded that that she be able to take care of herself, especially when she was in emotional distress.

Stolorow et al.'s (1987) thesis is that "selfobject functions pertain fundamentally to the integration of affect into the organization of self-experience, and that the need for selfobject ties pertains most centrally to the need for attuned responsiveness to affect states in all stages of the life cycle" (p. 67). Their view of the selfobject function is, of course, based on Kohut's (1971, 1977) revolutionary discovery and conceptualization of the mirroring and idealized selfobjects. They have, however, expanded the selfobject concept beyond the particular mirroring and idealizing ties and refined it by defining its function as the integration of affects and the need for attuned responsiveness to affect states throughout life as opposed to an overgeneralization of this concept encompassing "almost any care-giving activity that a child or developmentally arrested adult may require" (Stolorow et al., 1987, p. 66). Thus, Kohut's discovery of phase-appropriate mirroring of grandiose-exhibitionistic experiences is refined by "the critical role of attuned responsiveness in the integration of affect states involving pride, expansiveness, efficacy and pleasurable excitement" (p. 68).

CLINICAL EXAMPLE OF ATTUNED RESPONSIVENESS

In terms of the ideas presented in connection with "emotional availability," such attuned responsiveness can take many forms of expresssion. For instance, with one patient, Mr. C, whose hobby is playing the guitar and writing songs and whose keenest sense of intense pride, expansiveness, excitement, and authenticity are connected to music and only secondarily to his job, our discussions of various guitar heroes and songwriters has played an immensely important role in diminishing his sense of shame and increasing his ability to publicly play his own compositions. He has brought me CDs to listen to, and on one occasion I loaned him a Bruce Springsteen DVD. He was appreciative but also critical of Springsteen. In interpreting the meanings of these exchanges, we were able to discuss the belittling lack of interest expressed by his parents in regard to an activity they considered culturally substandard and irrelevant in face of "real grown-up duties and achievements." His own attitude toward his hobby and his job reflects this view. In treatment, this took the form of his feeling embarrassed about the relevance of his hobby in view of the serious issues he felt should be the topic of a serious analysis. I immediately had understood how important this seemingly unimportant topic was for his sense of shame around displaying an authentic sense of excitement about himself. His shyness and the deprecating manner in which he first talked about his music were what alerted me. We were able to discuss what it meant for him to lend me the CDs and also to listen to one of my favorites. For him, it was important to share an affective state of excitement with me while also being able to delineate from me in the form of differing musical tastes. Being critical of me was immensely difficult for my patient. His father was given to sudden bursts of violent rage, and his mother had a very strict code of conduct. He has a tendency to relativize any personal opinion he offers. We were, therefore, able to make good use of our musical exchange to discuss issues of compliance and the sense of danger he felt in exposing his enthusiasm and in offering me his views and music as well as in being critical of mine. Fittingly, he found Springsteen too bombastic onstage, implicitly a cautionary hint to limit my "stage" presence. At the same time, I must confess to remnants of unease in my reactions. Was I taking up too much space in my own enthusiasm about music? Was I satisfying too many of my own needs? Was I "acting out" in the sense of foreclosing a purely symbolic understanding of his feelings by listening to his CDs and lending him my DVD? I think not for the many reasons I hope to have made clear by now and, in particular, by the amount of analytic gain—the furthering of the unfolding of the patient's subjective world—that was the result of our interactions and the discussion of their multiple meanings. Nonetheless, it's another relevant example of the hold of the "inner circle." However, I feel that, as analysts, we have to stop behaving like schoolboys who pull up their white socks when the headmaster comes around the corner. A little more forthrightness and a little less looking over our shoulders about how we practice would be liberating. Does this mean that my practice is like a bazaar where the currency of emotions will allow any behavior? Does it mean that I would start chewing on a drumstick in the middle of a session? Certainly not. As a matter of fact, I object to my French analyst's behavior, with all due respect for the importance of food in France. At the time, I felt that it was disrespectful of him, and I felt that he impinged on my boundaries, but in my young man's fog of feigned indifference, I was unable to protest. My point is that, in treatment, we often say or do things that we come to fully understand only later. But within the usual ethical guidelines of human decency, we can't do too much harm as long as we always pay close attention to how the patient organizes how we are. Nor am I saying that anything goes or that the content and timing of our interpretations and actions are all equally good or to the point. With the understanding of our patients and their well-being as our central guidelines, we can perhaps learn to enjoy and make the best use of the inevitability of our subjectivity and live with the consequences it has for our patients and us.

Another example that comes to mind is my spontaneous reaction in offering a patient a "high-five" in answer to her prideful account of having achieved a difficult act of demarcation. I suppose this could be termed a "now moment" (Stern, 2004). It certainly served to highlight a moment of affective expansiveness. Both examples of affective responsiveness consolidated a sense of self-confident ambition and self-esteem.

I find Stolorow et al.'s (1987) view of the "importance of early experiences of oneness with idealized sources of strength, security, and calm" as indicating "the central role of soothing, comforting responses from caregivers in the integration of affect states involving anxiety, vulnerability, and distress" (p. 68) an especially helpful clarification of the function of the idealized selfobject transference. Kohut had also shown how important such an integration is for the development of self-soothing capacities, and Krystal (1988) has expanded on Kohut's idea of anxiety tolerance to explain the meaning of affect tolerance in general, adding his ideas to those of the theorists mentioned previously and to Stolorow's, in helping us understand the importance of affect integration for the organization of self-experience.

THE SELFOBJECT FUNCTION OF AFFECT-DIFFERENTIATING ATTUNEMENT: SELF-DEFINITION AND SELF-BOUNDARY FORMATION

Stolorow et al. (1987) then go on to extend their expanded concept of selfobject functions to "certain other aspects of affective development that we believe are central to the structuralization of self-experience" (p. 70). They expand on Krystal's (1988) idea that an important aspect of the development of affects lies in their differentiation and separation from a common matrix by pointing out that the caregiver's responsiveness in helping the child to perceive and differentiate between his varying feelings and affect states plays a pivotal role in "the progressive articulation of his self-experience" (Stolorow et al., 1987, p. 70). They describe this affect-differentiating attunement as a central selfobject function "in establishing the earliest rudiments of self-definition and self-boundary formation" (p. 70). The child will experience severe difficulties in his self-development, especially in the processes of self-demarcation and individualization, if the parent, because of a faulty structured sense of self and other, is unable to respond to the child's distinctive affect states. Self-boundary formation will be obstructed if the parent needs the child to fulfill his or her own selfobject needs and "feels compelled to 'become' the selfobject that the parent requires" (Miller, 1979, cited in Stolorow et al., 1987, p. 70). This will then be a central source of conflict for the child, as he or she feels impelled to sacrifice and dissociate his or her own feelings in order to maintain the tie to the parent.

To illustrate the role of the selfobject function of affect-differentiating attunement in the establishment of self-definition, I would like to return to Mrs. B, the patient whose traumatic background required an extended period of reexperiencing very early developmental states. In Searles's (1965) brilliant, detailed, and courageous descriptions of what is entailed for both the patient and the analyst in working with regressed states, he describes, on the basis of Mahler's concepts, what he has termed "the phase of the resolution of the symbiosis" (p. 543). He makes the point that either one or the other, taking turns, will initiate a shift toward emancipation out of the symbiotic phase, toward functioning as "individual persons, rather than (as) partners in symbiosis" (p. 543). In my words, rather than the language of Mahler that Searles uses, I had felt the impulse to bring more of her experience of the therapeutic relationship into the process.

Intersubjectivity theory would accentuate the mutuality of the shift, in other words, that the emancipation occurs as a product of the intersubjective field, as a shift in the relational field, rather than as a result of a sequence of unfolding stages. In our view of the analytic relationship as an indissoluble unit, it's more difficult to determine who is the chicken and who is the egg. Nonetheless, while we would avoid the universalization that a set sequence of therapeutic stages, such as Searles describes, entails, his language evocatively describes what it feels like to work with patients who suffer from early developmental arrest. The therapist will of necessity respond with "feelings at the level of his own early childhood experiences" (Searles, 1965, p. 537) as he or she resonates with the patient's feeling states. This means that he or she will experience very deep feelings toward the patient, feelings that can be confusing and scary for his or her adult self. In Searles's words, "I cannot overemphasize the extent to which it is the little child in each participant upon whom mutual trust must eventually be placed for therapy to succeed; in the Biblical phrase, '. . . and a little child shall lead them'" (Isaiah 11:6, cited in Searles, 1965, p. 537). This trust is necessary to balance the feelings evoked by the deep level of involvement of such work. Arriving at such a sense of trust is the reward for allowing deep feelings to occur. The child metaphor expresses the vanquishing of the "demons" we've met along the way. The boundless importance that the analyst has for such patients can evoke a gamut of emotions in the analyst: from omniscience fantasies of "unlimited potentialities for his own gratification" (p. 537) to feeling threatened in his psychological existence by the "unparalleled importance in the therapist's life, an importance . . . which he experiences also as a competitive threat to his most personal and cherished non-professional relationships" (p. 533). The felt threat—captured in the image of "demons"—is due to the depth of emotions, to the depth of the emotional availability required for successful treatment.

CLINICAL EXAMPLE OF AFFECT DIFFERENTIATION

My first clue to the fact that a shift was occurring was that in one session, where Mrs. B once again felt the entire extent of her self-annihilation, I made no move to buffer her pain, even though this session was before a vacation break. In retrospect, I must have felt we were both able, in varying degrees, to brave the threat of destruction. At the same time, I remember feeling very close to her in the stillness of the depth of her pain. Even though I was sitting some meters apart, I felt as if I were protectively emotionally enveloping her, that I was sharing her inner state. Her experience of personal annihilation had to do with her attendance at a party given by former colleagues where she felt that she was totally ignored. Not a single person had inquired about how she was doing and how she felt. If she wasn't part of their working world, then it seemed like she didn't exist. In fact, she had been told in so many words that her career was over. She said she felt completely vulnerable with nothing to offer. I said, "Yes you do, you have your vulnerability to offer. It's your former colleagues who feel that only achievement counts." After the break, she came back in high spirits. She said that being able to feel the depth of her sadness had been important and that my interpretation concerning her vulnerability had enabled her "to turn it around and feel rich inside." Someone had said that she looked like she was in love, to which she responded, "With myself, if at all." She had made the discovery that she could work and play, meaning that she could be good to herself and, by extension, that an integration had occurred between self and other. Work had meant subjugation to the other, and play had meant selfhood, which was insignificant. Her main objective now was to follow her own rhythm (she threw away her alarm clock) and to be whatever way she felt like being, trusting herself to work or play as the impulse moved her. She hadn't felt my absence as keenly as she had at other times, and she had fewer feelings of impending catastrophe. This was an "attack" on her old negative organizing principle, which required her to attend to the need of others while subjugating any wishes of her own. She was aware of this to the degree that she wondered and was somewhat anxious about becoming "arrogant." She'd always felt she was a "loser" and now felt unease if she saw herself in a favorable light in comparison with someone else. Her equation of feeling good about herself with being arrogant had to do with her feeling on the deepest level that any expression of her selfhood was destructive to the other. I had made this interpretation on various other occasions. This time it was sufficient to ask her whether she felt arrogant, to which she replied, No.

Both her parents had instilled in her, from the age of 3, that the highest virtue was to be rational, reasonable, and grown-up. As such, it was her duty to take care of and be responsible for her two younger siblings. She never felt that she was allowed to be a child herself. Her father, a scientist, had made an early claim on her, requiring her to follow in his professional footsteps, which she did. She was, in his eyes, also to be as smart as Einstein, as sexy as Marilyn Monroe, and as strong as King Kong. In other words, she was required to "become" his selfobject. Trying to halt the intersubjective chain of psychological events and extract the mutative moment that led to the shift is arbitrary and misleading to the degree that it excludes everything that preceded it and whatever may be expected to come. However, for the sake of argument, let's freeze-frame the moment. In this instance, my empathy lay in the fact that I initially withheld any outward response, with the exception of the "vulnerability" interpretation. At other times, it had been absolutely necessary for me to concretely intervene and offer a distinct countermeasure to her poisoned sense of selfhood, describing, for instance, the development of her progress. This time, I quietly held her sense of annihilation, thus signaling that she also was capable of holding these feelings. But who or what enabled me to do that? As her analyst, I may be the captain, but I can't float without the crew and the boat. In this example, the affect-differentiating attunement to her shifting inner states mainly took a nonverbal form. The accent here is not on her ability to develop autonomy but on her ability to feel a distinctive affect state as the basis of a new sense of self-definition. She was able to do this on the background of the safe space, cocreated by both of us, allowing her to experience her sorrow, and because her affect state was eventually articulated. Self-definition and self-boundary formation are established not by overcoming the need for the tie but by experiencing "ties that free" instead of "bonds that shackle" (Stolorow et al., 1987). I hadn't needed her to "become" my selfobject by mitigating and therefore subjugating her vulnerability to my fears for her well-being.

THE SYNTHESIS OF CONTRADICTORY AFFECTS AND THE INTEGRATED SENSE OF SELF

Another "critical selfobject function of the early caregiving surround concerns the child's synthesis of contradictory affective experiences, a process vital to the establishment of an integrated sense of self" (Stolorow et al., 1987, p. 71). This requires the presence of a caregiver or therapist whose own perceptions are firmly integrated and who can therefore tolerate, understand, and clarify that the intense, contradictory feeling states originate from a unitary, continuous sense of selfhood. If a caregiver or therapist needs to perceive the child or patient as "split" into one being whose "good" affects meet their selfobject needs and another whose "bad" affects frustrate these needs, then the affect-synthesizing capacity and the development of an integrated selfhood will be thwarted. The result is that the discrepant feeling states will become "sequestered from one another in conformity with the parent's (or therapist's) fragmentary perceptions" (p. 71). In the clinical example given previously, Mrs. B's "bad" sense of selfhood, symbolized by her ability to value her sadness and vulnerability, was allowed to coexist with her "good" sense of selfhood, symbolized by her ability to work. Her more integrated selfhood finds expression in her feeling that both states are a part of her self-experience and can be determined by her.

AFFECT TOLERANCE AND AFFECTS AS SIGNALS

A further affective development that is important for the structuralization of self-experience is the already mentioned "affect tolerance" and the "use of affects as self-signals" (Krystal, 1988). The ability to use feelings as signals to oneself also requires the parent's or therapist's attunement to the intense, shifting affect states. Their articulation, modulation, and containment makes this possible, and rather than experiencing affects as disruptive, they can be used to preserve the sense of self-continuity. In order to perform this selfobject function, the caregiver must use his or her own affect-signaling capacity. This will eventually become internalized, allowing the child or patient to use his or her feelings as self-signals. If this does not occur, then feelings themselves will be felt as a threat and will be repressed "or encapsulated through concrete behavioral enactments, self-protective efforts that literally cut off whole sectors of the child's affective life" (Stolorow et al., 1987, p. 72). Affects then become associated with experiences of shame and self-hatred, as they evoke memories of having felt rejected. Emotionality itself is then a sign of a terrible defect within the self, to be gotten rid of. Having feelings is experienced as solitary and unacceptable. Here the "discharge" metaphor attains clinical meaning. The patient who rarely had feelings in my presence and the role I played in her ability to feel safe enough to express emotion comes to mind.

I would like to return now to Mrs. B in order to discuss the role of the "desomatization and cognitive articulation of affect" (Stolorow et al., 1987).

CLINICAL EXAMPLE OF THE DESOMATIZATION AND ARTICULATION OF AFFECT

In the course of the months following the session described previously, the affect-differentiating attunement was more on the verbal level, and the processes of self-demarcation and individualization began to be more directly focused on our relationship. For a better understanding of the therapeutic process, some of the starkest traumatic occurrences in her life need to be known. When she was 8 years old, she was raped by two adolescents. She had been left alone and in charge of her two younger siblings in an unsafe place. She was able to save herself from the severest damage to her selfhood by disassociating during this horrible, traumatogenic experience. She has cognitive but not emotional recall of the rapes. She was also the victim of many beatings until she was 17. The violence perpetrated on her was within various sexualized contexts.

In a fairly recent dream, a cast-iron enclosure surrounding her burst open. She commented that she didn't need that kind of defense anymore. She has also been experimenting with various ways to feel more attractive as a woman and has begun to take note of men. Previous discussions of her feelings about being a woman were characterized by derogatory remarks concerning herself and men. She pointed out that she doesn't feel identified with being a woman. In particular, she feels that her sexuality is not a part of her; her "self" is "someone else." Sexuality understandably has to do with being misused and with severe injuries to her sense of boundaries and integrity. In the past, sexuality was the price she paid for affection and attention, for which she had to be thankful. It is closely enmeshed with violence and experiences of severe feelings of humiliation, panic, and loss of control. It is the opposite of feeling close to someone. Thus, sexuality is, for her, a concretization of not feeling lovable.

Our discussions about what it means to her and how it feels to be a woman led to the recurrence of intestinal symptoms that were severe in the first years of treatment but that have largely vanished. I asked her whether she thought that their reappearance had to do with the difficult topic of her feelings connected to being a woman. On the one hand, she didn't think the symptoms were "all that severe," but, on the other, she wondered whether this meant that she wasn't allowed to be 3 years old anymore. Being 3 was our shorthand for her long period of needing me to be the nurturing and affectionate mother. Affection, especially physical closeness, was not a part of her childhood experience. I seemed to feel more alarmed than she did by what I felt was a return to an "archaic, somatic mode of affect expression" (Stolorow et al., 1987, p. 73) and an unconscious appeal to me to contain feelings that threatened her maintenance of self-integrity— in other words, that a rupture in the selfobject tie had occurred that necessitated the remobilization of a psychosomatic state that represented an "archaic, presymbolic pathway of affect expression" (p. 73). I wondered whether she, in talking to me as a man about being a woman, didn't feel a loss of me as a motherly, protective, nurturing presence. She said she agreed in the sense that she sees me as a sort of positive mixture of mother and father but that she was also "curious" about the topic of her being a woman. In retrospect, I think we both felt, to differing degrees, frightened and curious. I asked her if she might feel scared about my reactions to our discussions of her feelings about being a woman. I felt torn between protecting her vulnerability concerning these traumatic issues and wanting to test the waters in terms of exploring what they might mean within our therapeutic relationship, and I said something to that effect to her. She responded by saying that whatever she experiences here in therapy spreads itself from the inside out, giving her a basic feeling of being okay in contrast to what she used to feel about herself. I responded by saying that I thought that was a whole lot and that it moved me. The first part of what I said was okay, but she reacted with a startled response to my feeling. That had been too much. By bringing myself into the picture, I seemed to threaten the selfobject tie, confirming some of what I had thought about her earlier psychosomatic reaction.

To my surprise, she came in the next day and said she wasn't allowed to move me because in her family she had always been responsible for everything that was wrong with them. In addition, her mother had many times told her that she had ruined her life. A very moving session followed this deeply felt recovery of a very basic negative organizing principle, the source of much of her rejection of herself, and much analytic gold came to the surface. To exist meant influencing another person, and this had always had disastrous, destructive consequences. In particular, she cited the one long-term relationship she had had in her 20s with a man 20 years older. This man had always had one main relationship and several other relationships at the same time, one with her as well. He had clearly been a father figure for her, extremely controlling but basically not able to commit himself in a relationship. When he, after 5 years, proposed that they move in together, she panicked and broke off the relationship. He told her that she had "destroyed" him, echoing the basic message she had received from her mother. For a long time, she felt this was the proof of her badness. We were able to explore that she had apparently given no weight to the circumstance that she was young and needed to move elsewhere for her studies or to the fact that he had not been faithful to her. Furthermore, on a deeper level, we were able to explore that she had freed herself from the repeated experience of having to subjugate herself in return for desparately needed affection as well as, albeit unconsciously, from her mother's stigmatization. She understood that she had equated being herself—having her own needs, wishes, and agenda, in essence, being alive—with being destructive. "I understand now why it has always been better for me to be an object." I said, "Yes, and just consider the implications of the alternative!" Understanding that I was referring to our ongoing discussion of her loneliness and her deep fear of ever being in a relationship and the implication that as a "subject" she could consider the possibility of having a partner, she shot back, "Yeah, to go on living with cats and dogs!" To which I replied, also playfully referring to her complaint of cat hair everywhere in her apartment and, by implication, to her need for an intimate relationship, "Too hairy!" Both of us broke out into loud laughter. This is a good example of the helpful aspect of laughter and exuberance in therapy.

In one of the following hours, I read her a description of a part of our work. I had earlier asked her permission to write about our therapeutic process. She had an amazing response: "I really do exist, after all! To hear this feels like proof that I exist." In retrospect, hearing the text proved to be a turning point in her analysis. The newly acquired sense of selfhood led her to be able to explore having a positive effect on another human being and, more frightening but exhilarating, the novel idea of having wishes or even making demands. She had needed this form of what I have conceptualized as "concretistic empathy" (Jaenicke, 2001) in order to counteract the crushing organizing principle that forbade her to be alive and damned her to remain the object of others. It would be hard to find better words than "I exist!" to describe the therapeutic effect of empathy. Being emotionally available and comprehending, modulating, holding, and articulating the ever-shifting emotional states of our patients may be hard work, but how rewarding it is when all the pain has burned off and just the beauty of being alive shines through the eyes.

The idea that analysts have no selfobject needs is another item for the myth list. The need to be effective in our work and the powerful effect of being needed are good examples. I was obviously very alert to any responses that my patient may have had in connection with writing about her. For instance, did she feel that I was distancing myself or, worse, using her? Clearly, her past pattern of pathological accommodation was more than reason enough for such vigilance. My feeling at this point is that it has strengthened our sense of a common purpose and her sense of distinctness.

Returning for a moment to the role of the selfobject function of articulating affect states for the organization of self-experience, we can understand the importance for this patient to be able to verbally articulate psychosomatic states. Her traumatic experiences are partly encoded in her physical symptoms; another part remains dissociated. The empathically attuned verbal articulation helps the patient put her feelings into words, and "more fundamentally, it gradually facilitates the integration of affective states into cognitive-affective schemata—psychological structures that, in turn, contribute significantly to the organization and consolidation of the self" (Stolorow et al., 1987, p. 73).

Stolorow et al. (1987) make two points concerning the treatment implications of their expanded concept of selfobject functions and the integration of affects. When defenses against affect arise in therapy, it is due to the patient's fear or expectation that his or her feeling states will once again be met with faulty responsiveness. My patient's psychosomatic response was just such a reaction. The second point concerns the reactivation of the arrested developmental needs as they occur after the transference resistance and the damaging childhood experiences have been sufficiently analyzed. The analyst's ability to understand and interpret these new and fragile feeling states as they emerge in the transference will be critical for the patient's growth. In treating the remnants of early selfobject failure, the selfobject transference bond itself thus will play a curative role in the integration and transformation of the patient's emotional life.

In conclusion to this chapter, I hope it has become clear that emotional experience has come to occupy a position of motivational primacy in contemporary psychoanalysis. Our own clinical experiences offer us the most profound appreciation of the paradigm shift in psychoanalysis. The central role that context sensitivity has in the psychotherapeutic process leads to an understanding of the radical contextualization of practically all aspects of life.

NOTES

1. "Every so often we feel like running away from so much mental pain . . . we may find ourselves wondering 'who on earth made me choose this job'" (Momigliano and Robutti, 1992, p. 16).
2. Donna Orange (1995) prefers the term *emotion* instead of *affect*, as affect already implies a distance to feelings inimicable to the essence of our work.
3. "This apparent tautology is important only because psychiatric and psychoanalytic languages have attempted to describe and work with emotion as if it were a cognition or an instinctual derivative" (Orange, 1995, p. 97).
4. "Kvetching," much like "yammering," is a Yiddish expression for complaining.
5. For an excellent discussion of this, see Bergmann-Mausfeld (2000).

4

Trauma

THE THIN CURTAIN

We were celebrating. Celebrating the end of my girlfriend's midterm exams at the University of California. This was 1968, the height of the rock-love-peace-higher-consciousness-through-drugs movement. Like many of our contemporaries, we disdained the numbing effect of alcohol and preferred what we then thought was the consciousness-raising effect of other drugs—*Doors of Perception*, Aldous Huxley wrote (the rock group The Doors took their name from that title). We had smoked marijuana, and each taken one benzedrine tablet, an amphetamine.

We got into an argument. My girlfriend said she needed some air and went outside. She came back and laid down, complaining of a headache. Suddenly, she went into convulsions that rocked her entire body in a wavelike motion. Her eyes crossed. I panicked, not knowing what I was seeing, except that something was very wrong. We had no telephone. I ran outside, knocking on neighbors' doors. No one answered. I ran down the street looking for a pay phone. I wet my pants. I called an ambulance. I got a continuous busy signal. I called up the only person I knew who had a car. We drove her to the hospital. I held her in my arms. She groaned. I told the doctors about the convulsions and what we had taken. I was petrified. California state troopers lingered outside. In those days, any drug meant jail. The doctor said, "Serves you right." They pumped her stomach. They misdiagnosed her. They told me she would come out of the coma. It was just a matter of time. In shock, I let my friend drive me home. He said, "She'll be fine." She wasn't. I phoned her parents. They flew down in a private plane. She died 20 hours later of an aneurysm. The father, a military man, said she was a victim of her times. The mother said she had had a history of headaches.

For me, time stood still. I saw everything in reverse: what was light was dark, what was dark was light—like the negative of a photograph with no color. I felt like I was endlessly falling. I tried to continue my psychology studies, but in statistics seminars, the computers and the numbers left me bolting for the door, senselessness sucking at my feet like quicksand.

My girlfriend lost her life just when her life was beginning to flower. I was never the same. For a while, I was nearly crazy. A rip had been torn in the basic fabric of life. In retrospect, I dealt with the incomprehensibility of death by trying to challenge it. When someone you love is ripped from you in a matter of seconds, you try to deal with what can't be dealt with. The outrage. The utter helplessness. The irrevocability. No deals can be made. Your mind tries to wrap around it and slips from whatever isn't there, from what is forever lost.

The form that my battle with death took was to rage against it in a vain attempt to say that I didn't care. Driving, I ran a lot of red lights. I got thrown out of bars and parties for provoking innocent people. I was clinging to life by behaving like it wasn't worth a damn. I was denying death and my loss by offering my life. I tried to match its absoluteness by pretending that I had overcome my fear of mortality. I was denying the unbearable embeddedness of being that her death had so brutally exposed. I prayed obsessionally. I developed rituals, such as nodding at every funeral home I passed. I expected her to walk around every next corner, whether I was in California, or in Split, Yugoslavia. I simply could not believe it was true. She had died.

One moment of reprieve came the summer after her death on a boat traveling between Split and Venice. I was sitting on the deck, and the sun was setting. The engines were drumming. I fell into a trance. In my deepest despair, I suddenly felt a wave of love wash over me. I felt completely loved, and a tingling sensation of ecstatic warmth passed through my body. Grace.

Her family, bereaved and in shock, had initially been very kind to me. Much later I heard they blamed me for her death. My analyst said that I would have to live with some amount of guilt for her death for the rest of my life. Years later, I came to understand that an aneurysm is hereditary and unpredictable as to why and when it occurs. But the damage was done.

For 10 years, I walked a very narrow line. What I couldn't fathom was the loss of the basic trust in life. The obsessional symptoms that I developed were an attempt to sew together the threads that had been cut. For many years, I tread as if the floor I walked on could give away at any moment. I understood the basic fragility of life and how thin the curtain between life and death is. Here one second, gone the next, was my basic feeling. Over time, I rallied. When a well-known German sociologist said that he defined himself by the gaps in his self-experience, I felt understood. Over time, I even felt that a gift had been given to me in the sense that, over time, I understood how precious life is. And yet I still feel deep sorrow for her, for her life unlived, and for the loss of my basic sense of trust in life. I envy those who, when they say "See you tomorrow" to people they love, firmly believe this will come true. Way back in my mind, a little jolt sends a question mark rippling to the surface.

THE "NORMALS" AND THE "TRAUMATIZED"

Stolorow (1999, 2003) has written two seminal articles on psychological trauma. He describes how after the sudden, tragic death of his wife, he felt a total sense of alienation toward everyone and life in general. A chasm separated him from others. There are those who have experienced trauma and those who have not. Stolorow (1999) cites a traumatized patient who divides the world into two groups: the "normals" and the "traumatized ones" (p. 465). There is no going back. In a discussion after Stolorow's paper was presented, it was illuminating to hear the audience's response. Many contributors attempted to make the point that trauma can be healed. I understand their response as being similar to my own initial denial. Time and time again, Stolorow said, in effect, that no, it cannot—not in the sense that that basic sense of trust can be regained. Certainly, one can find one's way back into life, and cracks that hold broken vessels are said to be stronger than the original mold, but the crack remains. This is an important point to comprehend when treating patients who have suffered from psychological trauma. The clinician has to accept that which has been destroyed. Any attempt to equivocate will ultimately be experienced as a possible retraumatization.

This is a difficult point for therapists in terms of the risk of relatedness. He or she must make room for the incomprehensible. In a very real sense, this is a demand that can't be met. If we understand trauma as unbearable affect, affect that shatters the sense of selfhood, then it isn't possible to resonate with such a feeling. But one can understand that which is not understandable and accept it. Let's see how.

CLINICAL EXAMPLE

In my work with one patient in his early 30s, Mr. T's accumulated trauma had left him feeling forever locked out from human emotion. He felt that his innermost being was locked in a "concrete vault." It was only when I, after more than 300 hours, accepted that he felt forever imprisoned with no chance of escape and told him that I had failed him and that I couldn't get him out of the vault that he, in turn, finally felt understood. I had not wanted to accept his basic feeling that his emotional life was an irrevocable disaster; I had, in essence, unconsciously fought with him for many years in my denial of this. I couldn't stand it. Intersubjectively, the risk had been too great for me, and I had therefore blocked progress in treatment. I couldn't face his deathlike feelings for analogous reasons of my own. The question arises, What enabled me to finally accept his feeling of defeat? In retrospect, it was that I accepted and admitted to myself—and to him—my defeat with him. This helped him because he had organized my refusal to do so as a denial of his feeling, and he was right. Therefore, his "resistance" can be understood intersubjectively not as a primary resistance to accepting his own feeling of nonexistence—he was quite familiar with that—but as a resistance to my refusal to understand him. His response was one of relief because I had validated his innermost sense of selfhood. In essence, he indicated to me that we now had achieved some kind of baseline from which we could continue to work. My resistance to his defeat was simultaneously a resistance to my defeat in the face of my experience of death. So it becomes clear that I am still working on the issues of loss and mourning. Two points are worth making in this regard: First, it takes a very long time to deal with psychological trauma both in ourselves and in our patients. The risk of relatedness for me was mirrored in the inherent emotional difficulties in facing unbearable affect—mine and his—and in the resistance toward my patient. Second, such issues can't be pushed. You don't jump into chasms: one good reason not to force traumatized patients—or ourselves—into facing such feelings too fast or too soon. We go slow, we use a lot of rope and good ties on our way in, and we rest a lot. In studies of concentration camp victims and Vietnam veterans, one salient factor for survival was the close tie to another human being, proving once again Kohut's view of the existential importance of the selfobject milieu. The writer Jean Amery, on the other hand, could deal with the unbearable affect he suffered through torture in a concentration camp only by taking his life. Everyone who has experienced trauma is damaged, and some patch up better than others. How one deals with acute trauma depends on the accumulated trauma that went before, that is, on how thin the fabric was before the acute trauma occurred.

TRAUMA: UNBEARABLE AFFECTS

Let us return now to Stolorow's work for a theoretical understanding of the genesis and effects of psychological trauma. In their chapter on psychological trauma in *Contexts of Being*, Stolorow and Atwood (1992) state that the "essence of trauma lies in the experience of unbearable affect" (p. 52). They go on to say that what makes affect unbearable can be explained by neither the intensity nor the quantity of the painful feelings evoked by an injurious event. Pain, as I have cited Stolorow before, is not necessarily trauma. Developmentally traumatic affect states can be understood only in terms of the relational systems in which they took form. Only when the attunement in terms of tolerance, modulation, containment, and integration of painful and frightening affect states that a child needed from his or her surround is absent will such affects become traumatic (Stolorow and Atwood, 1992). However, as Stolorow (1999) points out, he realized that he had "failed to distinguish between attunement that cannot be supplied by others and an attunement that cannot be *felt* by the traumatized person because of the profound sense of singularity built into the experience of trauma itself" (p. 465, emphasis added). When I spoke of the crack in the vessal or the rip in the fabric of my sense of life, I was referring to what Stolorow has conceptualized as a shattering of "absolutisms" (p. 467), which are "the basis for a kind of naive realism and optimism that allow one to function in the world, [a world that is] experienced as stable and predictable" (p. 467). This leads to "a catastrophic loss of innocence that permanently alters one's sense of being-in-the-world" (p. 467). The shattering of absolutisms is the essence of psychological trauma. The feeling is that one no longer inhabits the same world as do others. One feels that noone else can possibly imagine what one has experienced. The worlds of the traumatized ones and the normals are the same but are "felt to be essentially and ineradicably incommensurable" (p. 466), hence the sense of singularity, estrangement, solitude, and alienation. As a result, the traumatized person will perceive aspects of life "that lie well outside the absolutized horizons of normal everydayness" (p. 467).

Fortunately for me, there were two sides of this perceptual coin. On the one hand, I felt that singularity. I felt that I was looking through fractured eyes, eyes that saw things as there and as gone, as existent and as vanishing, the crack in everything. The thought that accompanied me was, "If you only knew!" Sometimes I felt guilty of arrogance for my apartness. The other side of the coin had to do with what I described as the gift of my traumatic experience. When life wipes you out, pulverizes your automatic feeling of a right to exist, an expansion can occur, one that leads to a profound appreciation and tolerance for any form of life. This has been invaluable for my relationships and, in particular, for my work with my patients, as it has sensitized me to the slightest movements toward liveliness. It has given me a sense of trying always to strengthen what remains, unless, of course, as with the patient in the emotional vault, I get caught in the crack. What helped me then was to remember how profoundly we fail in life—all the time, we fail—and to remember that mostly we survive. There is a paper-thin wall between defeat and falling apart. Often they are experienced as the same psychological phenomenon. The acceptance of defeat without dissolution becomes the new fabric of belief in survival. Acceptance, like grace, is a relational phenomenon. The difference between trauma and the everyday vulnerability of life is that facing the abyss forces you to feel the necessity of the tie that holds you. The loss of the belief in the tie is the abyss, and the abyss proves the need for the tie. We always live with both, but in trauma the belief is shattered, and we endlessly fall.

TRAUMA AND PAINFUL REACTIVE AFFECTS

When I speak of how thin the fabric was before the injurious event, I am referring to the effect of the accumulated trauma that occurred throughout childhood. If a child's emotional and perceptual experiences have consistently been invalidated, then his or her sense of reality will be fragile and vulnerable to dissolution (Stolorow et al., 1987). To restore the shaky belief in the validity of his experience and as a last-ditch countermeasure against fragmentation, delusional ideas might be developed whose function is to dramatize and reify the endangered psychic reality. "Delusional ideas were understood as a form of absolutism—a radical decontextualization serving vital and restorative defensive functions" (Stolorow, 1999, pp. 466–467). In my case, the obsessional behavior served the same function. The praying and the ritualistic behaviors I developed during that time were an attempt to regain the safe ground of absolutist belief. The sameness and consistency of the rituals served to regain a sense of stability and predictability in face of the horrible randomness of a totally unforeseen catastrophe. Chucking prayers into the chasm of loss dramatized and reified the void that was threatening to engulf me.

For both states—the discrete, dramatic, traumatic events and the accumulated trauma—what is salient for the genesis of psychological trauma is whether a person's painful reactive feelings are responded to. In many cases, the person inflicting the pain will not be capable of dealing with the reactive painful feelings of the one who suffered the injury. The inflicted person will then, in order to maintain the existentially necessary tie, explain the trauma as a defect in his or her selfhood (Stolorow and Atwood, 1992). Thus, when the doctor, the family, and the analyst were unable to deal with my reactive pain, I assumed that they were correct and that the cause of my girlfriend's death lay buried in a basic fault of my selfhood: had I reacted quicker, more knowledgeably, and more courageously when facing antagonistic doctors and policemen, she would have lived.

My mother's stipulation that I didn't have "the right stuff, like my older brother" was reactivated and exploded inward, spreading its poison. My counterphobic challenge in risking my own life in the aftermath can be understood as an attempted antidote to a crushing organizing principle. The suicidal aspect mirrors the lack of self-worth, while the rage, albeit also in the service of denial, was an attempt at self-righting.

In the process of writing this chapter on trauma, a question has arisen as to whether I have fallen prey to universalizing and reifying a psychological state. When one thinks back to my description of the life philosophy of intersubjectivity theory, such as that everything hangs on a thread, one could certainly get the impression that I have universalized my traumatic experience. Clearly, my subjectivity and my affinity to this particular theory are closely enmeshed. How could it be otherwise? Trauma exposes the vulnerability of the "unbearable embeddedness of being" (Stolorow and Atwood, 1992, p. 22) in a brutal way. The sustaining absolutisms of everyday life that are formed in a good-enough early childhood are a necessary prerequisite to be able to deal with the inherent vulnerability of being, while their intersubjective nature simultaneously encompasses and demonstrates the possibility of sustenance and loss. However, as we have seen, in the most extreme form, such as delusions, absolutisms are decontextualizations that serve a defensive function. As stated repeatedly, it is in the contextuality of human development and existence that the basic vulnerability of being lies. Trauma is an example of a dramatic loss of our belief in the possibility and necessity of being embedded. Ironically but understandably, sometimes intersubjectivity theory, in its attempt to deuniversalize and contextualize psychoanalytic theory, is criticized for robbing the clinician of absolutized belief systems. Replacing technique with practical wisdom, objectivity with subjectivity, and the metapsychology of drive theory with the intersubjectivity of affect theory, the contextualization of intrapsychic phenomena evokes responses of fear inasmuch as we can no longer find shelter in absolutes.

TRAUMA DESTROYS TIME

We have seen how trauma shatters the sense of our experiential world, robbing us of those absolutisms that allow us to feel that the world is a safe, predictable place and that our sense of self is inviolable. Stolorow (2003) adds another dimension of this shattering by exploring how trauma breaks the flow of time. It freezes the traumatized person in an everlasting present state of horror. The incomprehensibility of unbearable affect locks, shocks, and freezes the person in a traumatic state and, because there is no way out, also in time. The past becomes the present, and the future becomes meaningless. The three-dimensionality of time collapses, and our sense of coming from somewhere and heading to someplace vanishes. Our experience of stretching along time between birth and death, which "makes our existence fundamentally historical and thus meaningful" (p. 160), is eradicated: "trauma destroys time" (p. 158). Thus, one important underpinning of our sense of cohesion is knocked out: the unifying sense of selfhood as it is expressed along the continuum of time is shattered. To a lesser degree, we can see this same phenomenon when some of our patients lose their sense of cohesion over the weekend or after interruptions in treatment, such as vacations. By breaking up the unifying thread of temporality, trauma "fractures one's sense of unitary selfhood" (p. 160). A hallmark of progress when working with traumatized patients is when the flow of time becomes restored.

Mrs. B's reaction to the terrorist attacks of September 11, 2001, was clearly visible in her face: she had the expression of the haunted, shocked near annihilation of the traumatized. Her identification with the victims validated her own sense of destruction. She felt that now people could perhaps understand her. The endless repetition of the infernal impact of the airplanes into the twin towers became a horribly exact depiction of the time-looping effect of trauma.

Her reaction to the London terrorist bombings in 2005 was different. It didn't confirm her sense of the world as traumatic. She wasn't shaken to the core. But it did raise the question of whether the world wasn't a bad place after all. Just the day before, she'd been delighted by the newborn baby of a friend, spending a joyful, moving hour of easy interchange with the infant. This experience was in direct contrast to a deeply embedded, crushing organizing principle that children were nothing but a plague, as she had been told over and over again, leaving her feeling defective, unfit, and frightened of becoming a mother. Her mission in life was to remain single and to dedicate her life to science. By remaining childless, she was to remain bound to childhood; a sense of adult selfhood was allowed only within the narrow corridor defined by her father's vision of who she was.

The experience with the baby encoded the possibility of a different version of her as a woman whose sense of continuity into the future had become symbolized by her wish to be a mother. It was the implied possibility of even having a future that was new for her and that was not yet stabilized enough to not be somewhat shaken by the random attacks and disregard for human life demonstrated by the terrorist attacks in London. Nonetheless, the new experience of selfhood with a future represented a move away from the catastrophic, doomsday feeling so often described by the traumatized.

Mr. T's sense of being stuck in time is expressed in his basic feeling that his life is not going anywhere. He feels like he's just treading water; he might one day be able to afford a "really expensive watch," but nothing ever really changes for the better, and nothing matters. The future and the present have been sucked up by the vortex of his dismal past. Bleakness is the basic condition, and blandness is the code of the road. His life may look like it's moving, but he feels like he's standing still. His own words describe his history of parentification: "I was born an adult." If a child's selfobject needs for affective attunement remain consistently unmet, he or she will eventually withdraw to a vacuum-packed state of needlessness that matches exactly his or her surround. It is the only way to stay sane in order not to break apart on the rock of discrepancy between his or her perception of the world and the way the world presents itself. It is as if the child says to him- or herself, "If you give me nothing, then that's what I will become." As if by becoming invisible, it hopes to be seen.

DEVELOPMENTAL TRAUMA

Stolorow and Atwood (1992) conceptualized developmental trauma schematically as a form of severe disregulation that occurs in two phases in the child–caregiver system of mutual regulation. Unmet primary selfobject needs are rebuffed, producing a painful emotional reaction. The child then experiences a secondary selfobject longing to have those painful feelings responded to, held, and modulated. If these, as pointed out before, are again ignored, the child feels that these needs are toxic to the caregiver and must be hidden away in order to preserve the existentially needed bond. Children are survivors; thus, they choose the lesser evil. Nonetheless, these painful, walled-off feelings remain the source of lifelong conflict and are the basis of vulnerability to traumatic states. Thus, the need to constantly dissociate from painful affect will eventually provide the child with a protective cocoon where he or she will feel safe from the potential injuries that would result from longings for attachment to others. The price, however, is high: the walls that keep the injuries out also keep the child entombed in a vault of no feeling. Cut off from feeling him- or herself or others, time stands still.

Thus, in treatment, Mr. T often remains speechless. If asked what is happening, he will say, "Nothing." Part of that response is due to the fact that the absence of validating attunement, which "lies at the heart of psychic trauma" (Stolorow and Atwood, 1992, p. 55), has led to the patient's inability to read his own affect, so therefore he does not know what he feels or, in a more general sense, doubts his own reality altogether. The other reason is that feeling anything is experienced as a renewed invitation to trauma: either by being rejected once again or, intrapsychically, by becoming traumatically overwhelmed. For the therapist, it is of utmost importance to recognize the existential need not to feel. In terms of the risk of relatedness, the therapist has to deal with his or her own reactions to bouncing off the walls of the vault. My feelings of helplessness with Mr. T awakened my own deeper layers of experiences of rejection and insignificance. Anger against his "resistance" to my sense of efficacy or need to be healing is understandable but profoundly beside the point.

With both patients, Mrs. B and Mr. T, their sense of deep pessimism, their prolonged lack of hope, was the only way they could protect themselves or uphold a fragile sense of selfhood because, in effect, these patients blame their "own reactive states for the injuries that produced them" (Stolorow and Atwood, 1992, p. 55), feeling that their "unmet needs and emotional pain are expressions of disgusting and shameful defects in the self" (p. 55) that necessitate being banished from their conscious experience. Even after years of treatment, Mr. T will insist that his life is devoid of any occurrence worth mentioning, only to tell me, within the safe confines of the last 10 minutes of a session, about a significant event in his life. The thought of actually having a child explodes the perimeters of Mrs. B's sense of safety—an expansion of selfhood in time she can't dare to imagine.

CLINICAL EXAMPLE

In my work with a patient in her 40s, Mrs. R, the question has repeatedly arisen as to whether she suffers from the lasting effects of physical, sexual abuse. She has no direct memories of such discrete events. She is, however, flooded by pictures of violent invasiveness, some of which are clearly sexual. Recently, she was able to capture these flashbacks in drawings that she showed me. One drawing depicts a young girl with eyes widened by a look of terror and hair standing on end. Other drawings include pictures of snarling dogs; a screaming, angry man with an exposed penis; army boots crushing a girl; swastikas; and an ejaculating penis. Aside from the clearly sexual content of the pictures, what is striking is the fascist imagery of threat, oppression, and annihilation. The patient has until recently had a symbiotic tie to her father, a successful professional man who has supported her financially at critical junctures in her life and who promised to leave her enough funds to cover her pension needs. The father made it clear that the support was conditional. In return, she always felt obliged to try to meet his high standards of achievement and to comply with his narcissistic use of her. Her role was that of the supplicant. In childhood, he beat her intermittently, and she lived in constant terror of his sudden and unpredictable outbursts of rage. Aggressive tension, feeling controlled, and an injunction against being herself characterized the family atmosphere she grew up in. Placating her father and protecting her siblings were main concerns during childhood. He disrespected the subservient and depressed mother and eventually divorced her. The narcissistic use of the daughter included a highly eroticized component. The manner in which the beatings were carried out had strong sexual connotations. Other forms of physical contact were experienced "to be out of context" for the patient. Although there was no sexual abuse that she can remember, emotionally the patient, in effect, was assigned the role of substitute partner.

Mrs. R suffers from a constant fear of being invaded. Somatically, this is expressed, for instance, by her feeling overwhelmed by the noises of the city or by the negative vibrations of a hostile neighbor. The most deleterious effect of her fear of invasiveness has been a lifelong inability to form lasting attachments. It took several years before we were able to engage in a long-term, high-frequency treatment. At times, she would be flooded with images of blood and knives on her way to my practice. It is a testimony to her courage and her perseverance in her attempt to find relief from severe psychic pain and to establish a life of her own that she has been able to form a stable tie with her analyst. Mrs. R is a highly intelligent, sensitive woman, endowed with many talents. She has successfully pursued several careers but has not been able to identify sufficiently and long enough with any one career. As a result, she lives in a constant state of emotional and financial insecurity. We have been able to understand that this is partly due to her fear of being fixed in any one place: feeling targeted for invasion, she has to remain moving, keeping her true identity unclear. On another level, we have understood that if she were to become truly independent, she would rival and therefore lose her father. Losing the tie to the father would entail a primary loss of motivation and identity, her self-worth having been entwined with her ability to sacrifice herself in her attempt to gain his love. This, in turn, means facing areas of profound neglect and the terror of meaningless emptiness.

Treatment has progressed to the point where she no longer needs to primarily please her father. On a recent visit, she managed the previously impossible, highly significant feat of meeting him without dressing up. In her words, "Not dressing up was the external symbol of a felt sense of equanimity and self-worth in his presence. The great father figure had lost his omnipotent influence on my life. He's just an old man now." In the past, her relationships with men have largely been brief, characterized by sexually highly charged encounters, centering around the issue of submission or dominance. They encoded the relationship with her father in that she was simultaneously attracted and repulsed by sadistic, dominant, narcissistic men whom she ultimately tried to please, placate, and hold on to by her submissiveness. The masochistically colored mode of relatedness encodes both parental relationships. The father, however, has played a larger role in our work because even though this tie was based on a usurpation of a part of her personality, it provided her with a minimum of psychological sustenance and allowed her to escape the annihilating pull of a depressed and controlling mother. The sexual enactments were an attempt to be seen and finally valued by a man, while the excitement provided a buffer to those parts of her that felt profoundly abandoned and empty. With the significance of the relationship to her father moving into the background, a raw confrontation with feelings of depletion and emptiness has come into the foreground. These feelings evoke extremely painful experiences of near fragmentation. She counters these feelings with suicidal ideation, which she associates with her depressed, suicidal mother. She is, however, as she pointed out, able to differentiate between herself and her mother in terms of seeing suicide as a viable solution for herself, recognizing the symbolic function of suicidal thoughts as a relief from pain. Her main question now is who is she, if she is no longer identified with a defensively grandiose father or a psychologically self-annihilating mother. Although a certain amount of reconciliation with her mother took place before her death, the search for her own identity as a woman will very likely involve a further confrontation with her relationship to her mother. She feels that, if anything, it will be the tie to the analyst that will allow her to deal with this very bleak and, at times, hopeless period in her life.

After having painted a picture of Mrs. R's therapy in the broadest brushstrokes, I would like to retrace our steps. I will try to describe how her therapeutic process is reflected in terms of the most salient features of our mutual regulation in the intersubjective field. Her fear of "being fixed in one place" also applied to her fear of entering an ongoing analysis. Mrs. R has a long and varied experience of diverse forms of therapy, most of which were certainly helpful to her. However, their common denominator was a lack of an ongoing, uninterrupted deep attachment to the therapists. Initially, our work proved to be no exception. In hindsight, we carried out a struggle to commit to one another. She understandably felt afraid of being once again usurped, controlled, and exploited. I felt the need to set limits and boundaries. Generally, I do not see myself as a therapist devoid of flexibility, so I was puzzled by finding myself being quite "strict" with Mrs. R concerning issues of the analytic frame. She frequently called between sessions, wanting me to answer a question or change an aspect of our formal arrangements. Again I found myself largely unwilling to correspond. I had a sense of weariness connected to what I felt was a tiring battle to establish the basic terms of working together, and this contributed to our joint sense of uncertainty.

Joseph Lichtenberg's (2005a) concept of "wearing the patient's attribution" is helpful in explaining what was in our way. "Wearing the patient's attribution" entails understanding who we are for the patient. To do this, we must allow our own reactions to the patient to unfold in order to become aware of them. In terms of the risks of relatedness, this means accepting a view of ourselves that we might find painful or, frequently, foreign. For Mrs. R, I was the oppressive, dictatorial father, setting down the rules of our relatedness. In her phone calls, she would ask for a change in arrangements that were specifically tailored to her momentary needs. At the same time, she would usually end the call by making clear to me the extent of her sacrifices in upholding her end of the relational commitment. This posed an emotional dilemma for me: if I refused, I felt like a tyrant; if I agreed, I felt like I was concurring with her view of our relationship, as one in which she had to sacrifice herself. I now have a different understanding of the function of her calls. For, in fact, Mrs. R felt flooded by her fears of the encounters with me. She would have images of the floor of my office covered with blood and told me she felt the impulse to bring a knife to our sessions. The calls were an attempt to balance an existential fear of annihilation should she allow herself to become attached to me on what she felt were my terms. This is what she was trying to avoid by setting her own terms in order to protect a crumbling sense of self-integrity. In a sense, I was being pulled into an enactment. "Residues of traumatic lived experiences result in the patients cuing their therapists into assuming roles such as dominator-submittor, victimizer-victim, omnipotent-powerless, intimidator-fearful, seducer-seduced, abandoner-abandoned, intruder-invaded. Alternately, therapists can unwittingly cue patients towards roles of overcompliance, rebelliousness, dependence, or neediness" (Lichtenberg, 2005a, p. 107).

Formerly, Lichtenberg (2005a) explains, enactments were understood as a countertransference failure on the part of the therapist by allowing him- or herself to become enmeshed. His approach values the exploration of the verbal-affective message as much as the nonverbal implicit enactive-affective message. This view, much like intersubjectivity theory, is informed by the inevitability of mutual regulation, including being "pulled into an enactment unaware of the enmeshing cuing and responding" (p. 107).

Let us attempt to explore further what was guiding my need to be "strict" with Mrs. R. On one level, it was a legitimate response to her history of a lack of self-boundaries and object boundaries. Because of the many infringements, traumatic boundary violations, and usurpation of her sense of selfhood, Mrs. R has difficulty differentiating what she feels and what the other feels, particularly if it entails a conflict between her own agenda and the needed tie. Therefore, a part of my affect-regulating task has been to disentangle self and other experiences and self and other needs. In our work together, I have learned to be initially quite concrete in pointing out the various differences, only to, at a later date, offer a more dynamic interpretation. By stating what she needs and what I am able to respond to, we are now able to work out conflicts of interest. This opening of a joint space where negotiation can be cocreated has become a novel and healing factor in her treatment. Thus, we have created a new intersubjective field in which we can simultaneously explore the old dominator-submittor, seducer-seduced, abandoner-abandoned roles of her childhood while trying to find a new solution. On another level, my role in creating the initial intersubjective field was due to my need to counter her fear of being *fixed* in one place, by my fear of not *having* a fixed place, the many moves of my childhood creating a need for safety delineated by staying put in a clearly delineated place.

Let us return now to the original question of sexual abuse that we are currently grappling with in treatment. "Images depicting discrete, dramatic trauma, whether derived from memories of events, fantasies, or both in some combination, often metaphorically encode [the] more subtle, recurrent interaction patterns involving pervasive emotional exploitation of, and malattunement to, the child" (Stolorow, Brandchaft, and Atwood, 1987, cited in Stolorow and Atwood, 1992, p. 54). The profound absence of affect attunement and integration in the original, parental intersubjective matrix, in particular to reactive painful feelings, leads to the necessity to dissociate painful affect from experience and to withdraw from all injuries that could result from attachments to others (Stolorow and Atwood, 1992). The history of the lack of attunement lies at the heart of Mrs. R's cumulative psychic trauma and provides the basis of her fear of attachment.

The question of whether actual, physical sexual abuse took place remains open. Certainly, the beatings she suffered were dramatic, discrete traumatic events. In showing me the drawings, Mrs. R was able to overcome her fear of a renewed rejection of her painful feelings. She took the risk of retraumatization by exposing a painful part of her self-experience that she had previously feared was a sign of a shameful inner defect. Commenting on my reaction, she said that what had been important for her was that I had reacted calmly, saying little more than "It's terrible." I was thus able to "hold" (Winnicott, 1965) her feelings and alleviate her fear of a repetition of early developmental failure. For her, the fact that I said "*It's* terrible" signaled that I was being completely nonjudgmental and thus relieved her of reactive painful affects of shame.

The significance of Mrs. R showing me the drawings lies in the fact that she established me in the transference as the "secondarily longed-for, receptive, understanding parent" (Stolorow and Atwood, 1992, p. 57), resuming a developmental process that allows an integration of previously encapsulated painful feelings and increasing the capacity for affect tolerance. The fear of retraumatization by the analyst, should he or she rebuff the remobilized, thwarted developmental longings or disregard the painful vulnerabilities in the transference, is the main source of resistance. *"To attribute the affective chaos or schizoid withdrawal of patients who were abused as children to 'fantasy' or to 'borderline personality syndrome' is tantamount to blaming the victim and, in doing so, reproduces features of the original trauma"* (p. 56, emphasis added). To explain "negative transferences and resistances in terms of intrapsychic mechanisms located solely within the patient" is a similar deleterious decontextualization (p. 56).

We must remember—and this is easier said than done—that a patient's need to wall him- or herself off from his or her own feelings or to cut off the longings for relatedness to the analyst is "*always* evoked by perceptions of qualities or activities of the analyst that *lend themselves* to the patient's fears or anticipations of a repetition of childhood trauma" (Stolorow and Atwood, 1992, p. 59, emphasis added). So, inversely, we can ask ourselves the question, What has made it possible for Mrs. R to allow these dreadful images to arise in treatment, and why now? The mere physical presence or the empathic interest of the analyst can be enough to evoke the fear of retraumatization, especially if the lack of attunement has been so profound that feeling itself heralds the fear of traumatized states. Nightmares, sudden rages, extreme startle responses, and flashbacks have been recognized as symptoms of posttraumatic stress. Freezing, numbing, blocking, and the "death in life" have been understood as ways of dealing with such symptoms (Orange, 1995). Panicky responses to any emotion and emotional frozenness can also be, according to Krystal (1988), adult residues of very early trauma. "Preverbal trauma . . . is the experience of overwhelming emotion, prolonged into timeless terror, suffered without escape and without help" (Orange, 1995, p. 91). If we combine the appearance of the images of sexually and physically abusive invasiveness of Mrs. R's drawings with the other symptoms she reports, are we perhaps dealing with an encoding of a preverbal trauma? Her feeling of having no skin; of noises, emotional, mechanical, and electronic vibrations passsing through her like ghosts that go through walls; and of being on the edge of falling apart could also possibly be an indication of severe trauma occurring at the preverbal phase of development. If good-enough early experiences of containment, attuned holding, and modulation of painful affect states lead to a sense of sensorimotor integrity, "a sense of one's physical being as inviolable" (Stolorow et al., 2002, p. 129), then the symptoms of violation could point to "the life-long impact of the early shattering of sensorimotor integrity" (p. 129). The imagery of sexual abuse, while at this point in treatment not based on remembered events, could also be a metaphoric encoding of a loss of sensorimotor integrity, the loss of "primal absolutism" (p. 129), in very early childhood. Mrs. R has commented that it would be easier for her if she could pinpoint the abuse: "If I can pinpoint the injury, I can heal it; if not, I'm doomed." Determining a discrete event would take her out of the amorphous hell of the unpredictable and unexplainable violence of her childhood. It would bind the unbearable tension and redress the feeling of lack of control. The possibility of integrating a discrete event would hold the promise of freedom. Her feeling now is, How can I beat an invisible enemy?

THE ROLE OF THE WITNESS

The explicitness of the sexual imagery certainly would point to actual sexual abuse having taken place. It is possible that as the feeling of safety increases within a deepening therapeutic bond, memories of sexual abuse may surface. From my point of view, the lack of sexual, romantic, or sexualized atmospherics between us could mean either that the patient doesn't feel safe enough yet to allow such feelings or memories to emerge or that, for her, the issue is not primarily, at this point in the process, about seduction or aggression in the service of dominance. Rather, it is about the depth of injury and vulnerability that robs her of a basic felt entitlement to exist at all.

Orange (1995) has made use of Alice Miller's (1990) work about childhood trauma to conceptualize a "selfobject experience of witness" (Orange, 1995, p. 136). It is the witnessing—a subcategory of mirroring—of a person's experience that gives it validity and makes it real. Miller makes the point that the outcome of severe child abuse depends on whether there was anyone in a child's life that was there to witness the child's pain. Otherwise, the abuse is experienced not as abuse but rather as a torture that must be endured. The child and, later, the patient often feel that they deserve such treatment and do not themselves feel that it is particularly cruel or horrible. In effect, they see it as normal. Miller goes on to say that mistreated children must, at least once in their lives, hear that it was unequivocally the environment's fault and not that of the helpless battered child. The only way this can happen is if someone believes the child. Countless times, I have pointed out to Mrs. R—to her great astonishment—that the way she had been and was now being treated was outrageous. On many occasions, we would retrace the stations of felt invasion in her relationships now, pointing out where the barriers had been run over and the boundaries transgressed. Rather than feeling the pain of a violated boundary, there would be holes in Mrs. R's self-experience. Such breaks in the temporal experience of selfhood can be attributed to dissociation but also may be the result of the repeated absence of a validating witness at critical, painful moments in a patient's life. The fact that Mrs. R allows me to be a witness to her painful feelings gives them the validity and meaning necessary for her to reclaim her history. Part of the resistance to remembering traumatic events is because the memory will include the fear of being once again left alone with these unbearable feelings, evoking fears of psychosis or self-destruction (Orange, 1995). Only the secure tie to the analyst will make it possible for the patient to "discover and to survive realizing—making real—the full horror of what happened to her or him as a vulnerable child. Part of the horror was being alone" (p. 139). Part of Mrs. R's present feeling that she "can't stand it" is due to the fact that for many hours of the day, in spite of the tie to the analyst, she is alone with unbearable feelings. As Orange points out, "The pain is brutally given, relatively unorganized experience . . . the patient . . . can experience raw pain but needs the responsive other to construe it, to understand its enormity and meaning" (p. 140). The need for the other is the condition for the experience of selfhood. Witnessing is the specific selfobject need of the other that validates the horror of mistreatment and allows the patient to recognize what happened to her or him and feel the appropriate pain. Just as "the child's conscious experience becomes progressively articulated through the validating responsiveness of the early surround" (Stolorow and Atwood, 1992, p. 31), witnessing allows the patient to remember. It therefore undoes dissociation and reestablishes a sense of continuity in time. It undoes shame, allowing a more positive feeling of self-worth. The upholding or the healing of traumatic states, just like the disintegration or maintenance of a cohesive self-experience, is a function of the intersubjective field, whether it be in childhood or in therapy. The traumatized person can never recapture the "primary absolutism" that is a neccessity and a given of a good-enough childhood, but he or she can reach a new understanding of the Janus-faced quality of embeddedness. We can perhaps understand that on the other side of loss lies a profound appreciation of the gift of relatedness.

5

Transference

It seems to be the fear of moulding the patient in one's own image that has prevented analysts from coming to grips with the dimension of the future in analytic theory and practice, a strange omission considering the fact that growth and development are at the center of all psychoanalytic concern.

(Hans Loewald)

"I believe I could fall in love with you," my patient Mrs. B said to me with a hint of mischievousness, fear, and courage in her face. Think of the transference as a symphony in which a distillation of relationships have been woven into various themes guiding a person's life, with now one theme, then another, dominating, depending on what the intersubjective context has allowed to be brought forth.

This chapter explores the intersubjective view of transference. It also examines this central psychoanalytic concept in terms of the theme of the risk of relatedness. We do not see transference as referring primarily to regression, displacement, projection, or distortion. Instead, we see it as part of the fundamental human striving to organize experience and create meanings. In other words, at the most general level of abstraction, transference is a psychological organizing activity. *In treatment, it refers to all the ways that a patient assimilates the analytic relationship into the affect-laden, archaically rooted configurations of self and other*. The transference is a microcosm of the patient's total psychological life. The analysis of the transference provides us with an understanding of the patterns that dominate his or her subjective world. So, while the transference refers to the unconscious organizing principles that crystallized out of the early formative experiences, it is an expression of the *continuing influence* of these principles rather than a regression to or a displacement from the past. This concept of transference as ongoing organizing activity widens the focus from a purely intrapsychic phenomenon to include the input of the analyst. As stated before, no transference expression occurs or can be understood without being in some way connected to the therapist. Transference can thus be understood only within the formative intersubjective fields from the past as they are elicited in the intersubjective field of the present and in regard to those that are anticipated in the future. This explains why a detailed examination of the events occurring within the analytic situation that evoked the patients' transference reactions is fundamental to understanding the transference. Patients are always moving either toward us or away from us.

If we view transference not as a biologically rooted compulsion to repeat the past but rather as an ongoing attempt to organize current experience, we will be able to more easily embrace the multiplicity of its dimensions. In order to illustrate some of these dimensions and also to distinguish the intersubjective view of transference from some of the more traditional ideas, I would like to return to a description of Mrs. B's therapeutic process.

One further point must be made in order to put this discussion within the framework of a more contemporary understanding of our profession. We view transference as a multidimensional concept, with two basic dimensions: the growth potential of the patient and the conflictual, resistive, repetitive, defensive organizing principles. Traditionally, psychoanalysis has paid more attention to the conflictual, defensive pole of the transference. More recently, psychoanalytic authors (Silberner-Becker and Amler, 2005; Stolorow, Brandchaft, and Atwood, 1987; Stolorow and Lachmann, 1980; Kohut, in Miller, 1985; Tolpin, 2002, 2004; Tolpin and Tolpin, 1996) have placed an equal amount of importance on understanding and working with those aspects of the transference that deal with previously derailed or aborted but now resumed growth. This previous bias toward psychopathology is understandable in light of the fact that we are dealing with people who come to us because they are in various forms of pain. Nonetheless, it has led to a neglect—at least in psychoanalysis—of how to recognize, conceptualize, and treat the growth potential of our patients. Recently, the various authors referred to previously have picked up on and elaborated a concept of interpretation originally introduced by Kohut that matches the two basic dimensions of the multidimensional conception of transference developed by Stolorow and his coworkers. When we are addressing the painful aspects of experience, we are making *trailing-edge interpretations*. When we are addressing the growth potential of our patients, we are using *leading-edge interpretations*. I will return to this concept at a later point.

Returning to the symphony metaphor, our therapeutic action will be determined by the transference dimension—the theme—that is currently being played in the foreground. The question we need to pose to ourselves is whether we are dealing with the patient's longing for a new selfobject experience, his or her hope for a resumption and completion of an arrested deveopmental process? Or are we being confronted with the patient's transference fear of a repetition of the original experiences of developmental trauma? This second dimension of transference is the source of conflict and resistance.

CLINICAL EXAMPLE

For a better understanding of the multipicity of the dimensions of the transference, I now return to the therapeutic process of Mrs. B. Right before my summer vacation Mrs. B had, with great trepidation, professed to having loving feelings toward me. She felt quite safe with these feelings within the protection of the analytic setting. Asked for her fantasies in connection with her feelings, she said that she didn't really allow herself to imagine anything more than feeling strengthened and good. I encouraged her to approach fantasizing in a more playful "what-if" spirit. She could imagine my cooking her a meal and then going out to a café to talk. Her sense of curiosity as to what kind of person I am was awakened. She added that she had no sexual feelings for me when I noted the intimacy of the fantasy.

After my vacation, she remarked with an edge of resentment that I looked rested and content with the world. While she felt that her loving feeling had been a support for her in my absence, it also became apparent that her awareness of what she lacked in life—intimacy and contact in a partnership—had become painfully clear. I was able to connect her resentment and feelings of deficit with my leaving her alone while I was off on a vacation, clearly having, in her mind, everything I needed, while she had comparatively little. As a child, her parents had excluded her from family vacation trips on one pretext or the other.

Consequently, she contracted the flu but came to sessions nonetheless. She refrained from wearing makeup or dressing up. She looked forlorn and lost and felt fragile, vulnerable, and needy. Her need to be comforted and held crystallized in a wish for me to place my chair next to the couch and put a hand on her head. I agreed. The next session she told me that the physical contact had stopped her feeling of free-falling and grounded her. A memory surfaced that she had clearly formulated in her own mind at the age of 5. Only children who are touched are children who are loved. In her childhood, there was, aside from violence, no physical contact with the parents. Only the younger siblings were held and coddled. At that early age she therefore surmised that she was not lovable—the conscious birth of a central organizing principle of her personality. "My mother really always did hate me and my father expressed his love for me only after puberty. He was prone to emphasizing his love for me in a way that I found somehow off. Obviously this love of his appeared only at a time when he felt that I began to be of interest for him."

My agreeing to her wish had "profound consequences" for her. She reasoned that by her own childhood logic, she must be lovable if I agreed to place my hand on her head. The process of reversal of a crushing organizing principle had been resumed on another dimension.Whereas the reading of my text had led to a fundamental awareness of her right to exist, we were now dealing with reemergence of early developmental needs. She also said that she used to feel that anyone who could see inside her would feel repulsed and reject her. "No wonder," she said, "as inside me were all the horrible feelings about myself that I had to hide." I reminded her how as a child she longingly watched her mother sitting on the edge of her siblings' bed as they enjoyed the physical contact that she never had. Mrs. B's comment is a precise description of the consequences of prolonged experiences of malattunement. In order to maintain the existentially needed tie, she had equated her unmet developmental longings and her painful reactions to rejection with a loathsome inner defect, an inherent inner badness. As a result, a psychologically highly damaging inversion, or confusion of insult with injury, occurred. She developed a *defensive self-ideal* (Orange, Atwood, and Stolorow, 1997) that was cleansed of all those feelings she had experienced as offensive for her early caregiving surround. In the past, when such forbidden feelings reemerged, they were a signal to her of her self-loathing and were accompanied by shame and a renewed effort to mask feelings of isolation and neediness with a desperate, omnipotent sense of self-sufficiency. Inasmuch as this identification with the defensive self-ideal represents an accommodation to the narcissistic needs of the parents, the attempt to maintain a bond through compliance leads to what Winnicott (1965) has called a "false self."

Her utterance of loving feelings set into motion a chain of psychological events we can now retrace to demonstrate the highly intersubjective nature of transference. The loving feelings, a product of the intersubjective field, allowed her to feel and express her neediness as well as her disappointment toward me. Acknowledging the cause of the break in the tie—my absence—reestablished the selfobject bond. This, in turn, allowed her to overcome her sense of shame and to show me her painful feelings by coming to analysis in a disorganized and vulnerable state. She no longer felt the need to uphold her defensive self-ideal and was able to show me an authentic, albeit vulnerable, side of herself.

What she was showing me was the the other side of what Kohut termed the "vertical split." In the vertical split, two states are consciously maintained and exist side by side. The patient alternates between the two states without being able to connect them. On the one side of the vertical split is what Orange et al. (1997) have reconceptualized as *defensive grandiosity.* In this state, the patient feels above it all, at times imperiously in need of noone and nothing. It is defensive because it serves the function of disavowing the painful, enfeebled states on the other side of the split. The "noisier" the defensive grandiosity, the greater the need to avoid, to disavow the often deeply frightening fragmentation-prone states on the other side. Anyone who has experienced the horror of crumbling selfhood can understand the need for the noisy cover-up. Arrogant entitlement is nothing but the flip side of a sense of empty nothingness. Mrs. B's defensive grandiosity was not arrogant or devaluating; rather, it consisted of a conviction of self-sufficiency, born of necessity in the crucible of her early environment. In coming to me, sick with the flu, disheveled, lonely, and in dire need, she showed me how painful it was to be her. In doing so, she gave me the opportunity to help her in her attempt to make contact with the painful feelings walled off on the other side of the vertical split. In working with the vertical split, it is important to wait for openings in the defensive grandiosity. One neither "punctures" nor mirrors defensive grandiosity. The first approach would lead either to renewed "pathological accommodation" (Brandchaft, 1993) or to defensive states of rage. The second approach would amount to a collusion with the defense, resulting in a possible addiction to the analyst's responsiveness.

Returning now to the two basic dimensions of transference, Mrs. B had to overcome feelings of shame in connection with showing me such painful states. That she told me how her mother reacted with hatred to her neediness and let me know how she herself felt repulsed by her inner state can be understood as an indirect testing of my reaction to her. The indirectness testifies to her fear. Gill (1982) referred to such allusions to transference feelings in extratransference material as the resistance to the awareness of the transference. Nonetheless, she was able to physically show me that her pain and my reference to her deeply unfulfilled longings toward her mother as she sat by her siblings' bed was a sign of my understanding such "shameful" longings and, of course, a reference to my moving my chair next to the couch—a reference that did not need to be made explicit for her to understand me. Thus, the ensuing strengthened therapeutic bond allowed an integration of previously disavowed affective pain and a lessening of the need for defensive grandiosity. Ultimately, our handling of her painful feelings, disruptions, and fears of disdain led

Mrs. B to expect understanding rather than disdain and allowed her to expose her primary developmental longings.

My sitting next to her was a revival of a hitherto repressed wish and the reemergence of an arrested developmental need. When I asked her what she felt, she responded by placing the knuckle of her thumb on her mouth and briefly pantomiming drinking or sucking gestures. Was this a temporal regression to an earlier psychosexual oral stage that she was unwilling or unable to renounce, or was it a defensive warding off of a later developmental genital stage?

Her statements about her lack of sexual fantasies about me—the power of the unconscious notwithstanding (I am a firm believer in believing my patients)—and an absence of sexual resonance on my part, combined with her fantasy of being fed by me (cooking her a meal) and the gesture of a clearly maternal need for the breast as a concretized symbol of an early expression of a derailed somatic need for mother's attunement, led me to be convinced that we were dealing with the reemergence of a very early thwarted developmental need. The lack of the early tie to her mother made her all the more susceptible to her father's eroticized expressions of affection. She was forcibly pulled to a later level of psychological organization that she had been unable to deal with, as she lacked the necessary maternal underpinnings of psychological structure. It is a testimony to the tenacity of the human spirit and to the basic need to organize experience that she would—given a facilitating context—grasp the opportunity to resume her development at the point that it had been arrested.

Her traumatic history of physical abuse and misuse made me extremely cautious and vigilant toward any wish of hers for physical contact. In hindsight, she had portrayed these early needs in the form of drawings of an infant being held in the beginning phase of treatment. She had also voiced the fantasy of the placing of my hand on her head at various junctures of the therapeutic process. I had noted these wishes but had not considered responding, as I had felt that neither her development nor the context called for such a response. Now, however, I felt that we were in sync with what was emerging in the intersubjective field. On the one hand her wishes and reactions and on the other hand my close examination of my transference feelings toward her, which had produced associations of early memories of the grounding and soothing effect of holding my own child, combined with the sense of competent security that my 3-year body-psychotherapy training had given me, allowed me to feel that we were on safe therapeutic ground. I thought that we were dealing not with the warding off of sexual feelings but rather the reemergence of an early need for psychosomatic attunement and closeness.

I am reminded of Kohut's case where, when faced with a severe suicidal crisis, he offered his patient his hand. He silently interpreted her holding his finger as if a symbolic offering of the breast was taking place. This earliest reenactment of the primal maternal tie was needed to counter the threat of annihilation the patient felt.

In a sense, this seems to be what occurred analogously with Mrs. B, not in response to an acute threat but in answer to a basic threat to her sense of selfhood. Her deepest feeling of being unlovable—"human junk" as she had put it earlier—of being defective had been encoded cell deep within her psychological organization of rejection and self-loathing. This annihilating organizing principle had resurfaced in connection with her wish for a second developmental chance within the analytic tie. We are working here with a very archaic mode of organization that, while reflecting a regression to an early stage of structuralization, was neither a temporal regression nor a displacement of an early representation of an external object. Rather, this level of structuralization has remained functional throughout the patient's life and was allowed to become salient in her organization of the analytic relationship. On the basis of this clinical example, I would like to describe some of the theoretical differences between the intersubjective and the traditional understanding of transference.

TRANSFERENCE AS REGRESSION

In the literature, *regression* has many meanings, such as topographic, psychosexual, structural, and genetic, to name a few. However, the concept is used in two general ways: regression as a retrogression along a time dimension and regression as a diminution in the level of psychological organization. Temporal regression poses several problems that can be avoided if we refer to regression only as a level of structuralization. Of course, archaic modes of psychological organization are related to the psychological organizations found in childhood, but we do not see them as identical with the manifestations in the young child. It is unwarranted to make direct inferential leaps from adulthood to childhood, for instance, such as when dependent clinging in the adult is described as a regression to a symbiotic phase of early infancy. Symbiosis, as infant research has shown, is not normative infant behavior. The need for disengagement is just as salient. Thus, what the adult wishes for may be related to an earlier developmental phase but is not identical to what a child wants. The reason it is important to make this distinction is twofold. First, we would misconstrue adult behavior, robbing it of its complexity. Second, and perhaps just as problematic, we might be tempted to make a judgment of our patients' behavior: slipping from our perception of our patients' states as child-related to seeing them as childish. This problem of a moral judgment becomes even more germane when we think of regression in terms of psychosexual development. If we view psychopathology as a temporal regression to an earlier psychosexual stage, then we are once again making the mistake of seeing the adult's behavior as identical to that of a child transversing the corresponding psychosexual phase. In other words, we mistakingly assume that an adult with psychosexual wishes and conflicts must be functioning like a child. The most deleterious clinical consequence of temporal regression becomes clear when we understand how it implies a maturational morality. The notion of the linearity of psychosexual development implies that in order for an adult to reach maturity, he or she must be willing and able to renounce earlier stages in favor of later ones. Therefore, temporal regression implies a failure in renunciation.

The work with Mrs. B can illuminate the pitfalls of viewing regresssion in terms of temporal retrogression. Had I understood her archaic need to be held as a failure or an unwillingness to renounce oral needs, I would have missed understanding the expression of her wish as a reemergence of an aborted developmental need. I would also not have been alert to the possibility that higher levels of organization, such as self-empathy, differentiation between self and other, humor, and perspective, could be revived—as they all were—and become a part of the work with the archaic level of structuralization.

Restricting the concept of regression to the level of psychological organization makes its relevance for the transference clearer. We are now in a position to assess whether archaic material refers to aborted, precluded, or disavowed states so that we can understand the reemergence either as a developmental achievement or as a means of warding off other material. In either case, our goal will be to promote integration, thus allowing a richer psychological functioning, rather than seeking elimination or renunciation. Thus, we cannot say that a patient has retrogressed to an infantile state. We can only say that archaic levels of structuralization have become revived in the intersubjective field, either in the service of defense or in order to resume arrested development. Analysts can be more alert to the possibility of attaining higher levels of organization. A shift can occur away from maturational morality toward growth potential. A subtle but significant alteration in our clinical sensibility occurs when we treat archaic modes as potentially enriching rather than pathologically burdensome. I would not be writing about the risk of relatedness if I did not understand and have empathy for the weighty aspects of treating archaic states and the concommitant temptation to avoid them, to give in to the pull of higher states of organization.[1] Once again, however, I must place the emphasis on the intersubjective nature of therapy. The patient bears the weight and risk of experiencing archaic states, while we carry the responsibility of responding to these deep feelings in our patients and in ourselves. I can readily understand the need to point the finger of pathology, but it begs the very intersubjective question of whether I am part of the cure or part of the disease.

TRANSFERENCE AS DISPLACEMENT

In the traditional view, emotions associated with an unconscious representation of a repressed object are displaced to a mental representation of an object of the external world (Nunberg, 1951). While intersubjectivity theory agrees that the transference gives the therapist an idea of how the patient organized childhood relationships, in our view of transference as organizing activity, nothing is removed from the past to be attached to a current situation. The understanding of the patient's past is due not to displacement but rather to the structures that were organized in the past that continue to be functional. The problem with the concept of transference as displacement is that it leaves out the influence of the analyst's activity or nonactivity. In the traditional view, the patient's experience of the analytic relationship is seen solely as a product of his or her past and pathology, whereas we view the patient's experience of the analytic relationship as always formed by both the input of the analyst and the structures of meaning into which they are assimilated by the patient. Leaving out the analyst's contribution places a "cordon sanitaire" around him or her that is reminiscent of how some patients have problems feeling or saying anything negative about their parents. In this case, we are the parents who insist ourselves on remaining within the safe confines of our therapeutic ivory towers.

The traditional reasoning for the quixotic attempt to exclude the analyst's contribution from an understanding of the patient's transference—a corollary to viewing the transference as emanating solely from the patient—is to avoid "contaminating" the transference. As stated earlier, the idea here is to avoid gratification of infantile wishes so that these "frustrated" wishes can emerge from repression, become symbolized, and be articulated. Here the rule of abstinence, that is, the active frustration of the patient's wishes and needs, is seen as part of the stance of neutrality. The question arises, In what way can such a nonaction be seen as a "neutral" act?

In contrast, intersubjectivity theory holds that any restrained action, nonaction, or action on the part of the analyst will profoundly affect the patient's reactions, codetermining which dimension of the patient's transference will dominate at any given time. In fact, the consistently abstinent analyst who ignores a reemerging developmental need will inadvertently repeat the patient's childhood experiences of malattunement, thus contributing "to the unconscious conviction that unmet developmental yearnings and reactive feeling states are manifestations of a loathsome defect or of an inherent inner badness" (Orange et al., 1997, p. 80). This is a good example of the potentially harmful consequences of neutrality and a clinical sensibility that excludes the importance of growth in favor of a bias toward viewing patient material largely in terms of defense resistance. The result may be that patients are willing to undergo years of deprivation in treatment because of the fit between shame, self-reproach, self-loathing, and the abstinent stance. This corresponds with the child-like interpretation that if something bad happens to them, they are to blame. As we know, a child explains unbearable affect as an affirmation of his or her badness. Thus, under the guise of promoting unconscious material through abstinence, a retraumatization may take place. The patient is left to "starve on the vine." If, as a result of an attitude of relentless abstinence, the patient reacts with intense conflicts over primitive hostility, which is then interpreted as a negative therapeutic reaction, then we are dealing with an artifact of the therapeutic stance. Then we would be adding insult to injury.

The question that is more germane to the treatment of archaic developmental needs is whether a therapist who responds to such wishes by actively fulfilling the patient's needs may be impeding the "development of more advanced modes of organization in the transference" (Stolorow et al., 1987, p. 42) . In my view, as can be seen in the case material presented in this chapter, it may be necessary to fulfill such needs or an essence of such wishes at certain times in treatment. While the fulfillment of needs does not preclude their analysis, at times the fulfillment must precede the symbolic analysis. It is a question of assessing the developmental stage as it emerges in the intersubjective field. Both the assessment and the resulting action are analytic as long as we conceptualize analysis as understanding the patient and reacting accordingly. Then we need not limit our conception of psychoanalysis to symbolic interpretations. We can include direct verbal and nonverbal responses, and a wish fulfillment can also be understood as an interpretation in a widened sense of this concept. The concreteness of a response may match the archaicness of the level of structuralization. It has been my experience that patients will and do signal shifts in their needs. Analogously, does a satiated baby not stop drinking? The fear here is that a patient will remain in an archaic state, analogous to a pampered child who sees no reason to leave a home that supplies all needs. While there is some truth to this in the sense that patients, like children, might feel ambivalent and fearful about moving forward, it is my experience that attunement to needs leads to growth and the impulse to expand. Ultimately, their expansion will break through and exceed the confines of what we are able and willing to give them.

What allows and leads patients to leave is that they have organized the repeated experiences of a good-enough fit between wish and response into a conviction of efficacy, of believing enough in themselves to try to get what they want in the world. Thus equipped, why should they stay "home"? Furthermore, as we also know from attachment theory, it is the securely attached person who moves most freely. In other words, it is the conviction of the possibility of the fit itself that gives patients the trust to disengage and reengage.

Of course, it is also necessary to nudge patients to higher levels of organization, for instance, by spotting the growth potential and articulating—through interpretation—their leading edge of development. Interpreting the trailing, defensive dimension may serve the same purpose. Nonetheless, my clinical experience confirms the intersubjective view of the patient and analyst as an indissoluble unit. Thus, who is to say in a discrete sense, if we do not revert back to Cartesian thinking, who prompted the next move? The clinical examples in this book show how closely knit patient and therapist reactions are. The mutual regulation of the therapeutic experience is so intricately entwined that the question we need to ask cannot be reduced solely to what the therapist must do or refrain from doing; rather, the question is, How did we get here, and what do we need to do now to further the unfolding of the patient's inner world? Therefore, intersubjectivity theory does away with the rule of abstinence and the corresponding concept of neutrality and replaces it with an attitude of sustained empathic inquiry (Stolorow et al., 1987). This allows us to assess what the patient may need through an understanding of his or her expressions within their subjective frame of reference and to respond accordingly.

FEARS OF THE THERAPIST

In terms of the risk of relatedness, archaic needs may evoke an archaic resonance in the therapist. Two points must be made in this regard. First, we need to stay aware of our own archaic needs for selfobject relatedness and our fears in responding to a patient on this level of structuralization. Once again, we can better understand the source of such concepts as abstinence, neutrality, and displacement if we include the intersubjective nature of treatment in our discussion of how we view transference. The depth of feeling that may be evoked in an analyst working with the force of archaic affects may be experienced as so intense that the analyst may become blind to the patient's need to move on. Or deficits in the analyst's needs for archaic attunement may be evoked by the patient's transference, tilting the scales away from staying centered on the patient's needs in favor of the analyst's. Here the analyst's need for attunement may get confused with the supposed need of the patient. The analyst's continued attunement on an archaic level is then either an expression of or a warding off of his or her own need for attunement.

Second, the fear that the patient will remain stuck on an archaic level of organization may cover up a fear on the part of the analyst that he or she will be either overwhelmed or inadequate in responding to such needs. The fear arises from the felt experience of being swamped or swallowed by archaic neediness. Working on archaic levels of structuralization may be experienced as a fear of dissolution between inner self and object differentiation, rattling the boundaries of our demarcation. The fear of inadequacy expresses itself as a fear of disappointing or not living up to the depth of the need in the patient. Here we fear that the necessity to engage the patient on such levels precludes our need to disengage from the patient.

If we understand transference, that is, how the patient experiences and organizes the analytic relationship, as a product of the input of both therapeutic participants, then we will need to track and understand not only the patient's responses but our own as well. So, in terms of intersubjectivity theory, transference is a two-way street. This means that our own transference is also a product of the intersubjective field. We can now better understand how the risk of relatedness explains one of the reasons for the notion of transference as displacement. Perhaps it is not so much that we fear "contaminating" a transference by our non-abstinent reactions but that we fear being "contaminated" by the transference of the patient. Seeing transference solely as an intrapsychic phenomenon, cleansed of our input, allows us to safely distance ourselves from strong emotions and the vicissitudes of entanglement that are part and parcel of mutual regulation and the intersubjective field.

TRANSFERENCE AS PROJECTION

Analysts who base their work on the ideas of Melanie Klein tend to conceptualize transference in terms of the mechanism of projection. Here transference is seen, for instance, as the projection of rejecting internal objects on the analyst, converting internal conflicts into external ones. Intersubjectivity theory defines projection as a defensive process whereby an aspect of oneself is kept from awareness through attribution to an external object in order to avoid danger and alleviate conflict. To restrict the definition of transference solely to defensive externalizations can lead to a neglect of other dimensions and meanings of transference. Projection may or may not emerge as an aspect of transference, depending on whether it is characteristically employed to ward off subjective dangers. Whether projection serves as a defense to ward off conflict depends on whether a minimum of self-object differentiation has occurred. In order for a translocation of mental contents across self-object boundaries to occur, those boundaries must be at least partially consolidated. If we are dealing with more archaic levels of structuralization, then the developmental achievement in self-boundary formation can't be assumed. Once again, this distinction is important when we are working with developmental arrests. In the case of undifferentiated states, the patient needs to reestablish an archaic relatedness in which he or she can resume the thwarted developmental processes of self-articulation and self-demarcation (Stolorow and Lachmann, 1980). If we misconstrue such a need as a projection of hostile feelings, we may feel attacked, make an interpretation centering on warding off a conflict, and thus inadvertently send the developmental need into renewed hiding.

TRANSFERENCE AS DISTORTION

In all the conceptions of transference discussed so far, there is an implicit assumption that transference involves a distortion of "reality." In this view, the present relationship with the analyst is warped by the patient's unconscious infantile past or "infiltrated by the patient's endopsychic world of internal object relations" (Stolorow et al., 1987, p. 34). This would place the therapist in the position of deciding what is "objectively real" and what is distorted. Judgments about what is "true" would then be left in the hands of the analyst, as if his own subjectivity were not filtering what he perceives and as if he had no stake in the matter—as if he were a disinterested party. I have discussed the pitfalls of this view in chapter 2. The point that is most germane to our discussion here is that this sets up a two-reality hierarchy of perception in which the analyst has the privileged vantage point of "knowing" what is objectively true as opposed to what the patient says he or she is experiencing (Schwaber, 1983). While I agree with Schwaber's critique and with her demand to relentlessly attempt to understand the patient within his or her own subjective framework (and I have read about and experienced her amazing ability to do so), I cannot agree with the implicit idea that one could expunge one's own subjectivity and attain an "immaculate perception" of the patient. We disagree with both positions insofar as we believe that "truth" is arrived at dialogically and is the product of both subjectivities involved. Our position is closer to Gill's (1982) critique of transference as distortion, as it implies that the patient's transference is solely an intrapsychic production. So, instead of thinking that we know better or that we could totally capture the patient's transference experience, a more accurate formulation than distortion would be to asssume that there are additional interpretations to the one the patient has reached. This stance saves us from being the arbitrator of some absolute external reality.

Transference, in our view, "is a sampling of psychic reality in purest culture" and belongs to what Winnicott (1951) called "the realm of illusion," an "intermediate area of experience, unchallenged in respect of its belonging to inner or external reality" (p. 242, cited in Stolorow et al., 1987, p. 35) . Just as we do not ask the child whether his or her transitional object was his or her own conception or whether it was presented to him or her from without, our analytic stance toward the transference does not pose this question about "reality." Our contextualist clinical sensibility allows us to understand that our present understanding of anyone or anything is "only a perspective within a horizon inevitably limited by the historicity of our own organized and organizing experience" (Orange et al., 1997, p. 89). It opens us up to the many meanings of a patient's experience and to the role that the intersubjective field plays in the cocreation of truth.

INTERPRETING THE LEADING EDGE OF THE TRANSFERENCE

Earlier I noted what I felt to be a bias in psychoanalysis in the past toward focusing on the defensive, resistive, conflictual pole of the transference. Insofar as we view transference as a result of the continuing influence of established organizing principles, as part of the patient's psychological organizing activity, resistance is also based on transference (Stolorow et al., 1987). Nonetheless, either the impulse toward new development or the fear of repeating the dreaded past (Ornstein, 1974) will dominate at any given moment in the therapeutic process. With the advent of Kohut's self psychology and intersubjectivity theory, psychoanalysis has been enlarged to encompass developmental needs and the role of selfobject functions. Thus, a shift has occurred in the focus of therapeutic treatment toward a more balanced approach of what is seen as deserving of our attention.

Correspondingly, the concept of interpretation has been widened and refined by the recent introduction of the leading edge in addition to the trailing edge of interpretations. In making use of this leading-edge form of interpretation, the analyst is called on to tease out the "developmental tendrils" (Tolpin, 2002) that patients offer us in their material. These "tendrils" are often hidden within defensive statements or mixed with more pathological states. The challenge for the analyst is to be sensitive enough to be able to pick them out. Such an awareness is given only if we are prepared to work with and enhance a patient's growth potential. One of the major hindrances to such a stance is the concept of acting out.

ACTING UP INSTEAD OF ACTING OUT

Analysts have embraced Kohut's work or allowed its spirit to influence their therapeutic practice and widen their concept of treatment to include interpretations of developmental needs, wishes, deficits, and growth. Nonetheless, the traditional juxtaposition of action versus symbolization and interpretation still has, in my view, a constrictive hold on what constitutes analytic practice. As Renik has pointed out (Symposium, Munich, 2005) this goes back to Freud's "Project" (1895), where symbolization and action were held to be inimicable.

Recent psychoanalytic literature (Lachmann, 2005; Lichtenberg, 2005a) on the importance of implicit and explicit communication and on the nonverbal aspects of treatment heralds a shift away from such a dichotomization. Thus, the concept of acting out has been replaced by the concept of enactment (Heisterkamp, 2002; Lichtenberg, Lachmann, and Fosshage, 2002) or by, now only in the therapist's case, a related concept, the wearing of the patient's attributions (Lichtenberg, Lachmann, and Fosshage, 1992). Rather than understanding acting out as an often pathologically tainted refusal or solely as a developmental inability to symbolize, we now understand such expressions of the patient—or the therapist—as just another form of communication.

Stolorow used to quip that the patient is acting up, not out. The analyst's task remains the same: to understand the meanings the patient is attempting to convey. In this regard, I find it most helpful not to categorize patient's expressions in terms of behavorial versus symbolized actions. Instead, we are called on to assess the patient's expressions in terms of the level of structuralization. Such a developmental assessment avoids the pitfalls of pathologizing the patient on the one hand and of unnecessarily judging and constricting our responses as possibly unanalytic on the other. We are then in a position—as I have repeatedly pointed out in this book—to answer the patient's material with a response that matches the psychological level that needs to be addressed. We can therefore widen the concept of what we conceptualize as interpretation to address a much wider range of the patient's expressions with a much greater variety of responses.

Let me illustrate this with the following analogy. If we were confronted with a drowning person, we would not point out to him that he needs a life vest. We would throw him one or, in extremis, jump in ourselves. Similarly, when faced with a crumbling sense of selfhood, it might not suffice to interpret a wish to be healed or held or to simply acknowledge the patient's fragile state, although all these responses obviously are a part of standard analytic procedure. It may be necessary to say, "You'll make it" or "I'm here and I'll help you" or "I am so sorry that it hurts so much." Another example would be that, in the face of a patient's reporting difficulties in overcoming severe obstacles in reaching a goal, it might not be enough to say, "You want me to understand how hard you've struggled," or to make a genetic interpretation. Instead, it may be called for to say, "That was courageous!" or simply, "Bravo!" In their important book *A Spirit of Inquiry: Communication in Psychoanalysis*, Lichtenberg et al. (2002) make the clinically invaluable point that "all our of our verbal communications, including exploratory and interpretive communications, contain intonations, metamessages (Wachtel, 1993), bodily and facial expressions, and possible attitudes of warmth or aloofness, of authoritarianism or collaboration, of acceptance or judgment, all of which contribute to the patient's implicit and explicit relational experience of the analyst. The *music* of our language (Knoblauch, 2000) as well as the content communicate our meanings" (p. 90, emphasis added). Time and time again, patients will point out the importance of experiencing our emotional engagement as a further indicator of being understood. In order to avoid a critique often justifiably voiced by patients, namely, that we are responding mechanically, we need to employ qualities of communication that are facilitative in personal relationships. Because we know that we are always revealing ourselves to our patients, we should recognize that, for instance, "warmth, friendliness, and personal openness" contribute just as "substantially to creating a facilitative therapeutic environment." The emphasis on the blank screen, anonymity, and neutrality has precluded their recognition within the psychoanalytic arena" (p. 91). The pall that sometimes covers analytic responses or even events and that is mistaken for seriousness or professionalism is an outgrowth of such a clinical approach. A patient's complaint that we may be treating them merely "professionally" may be a form of defense against their own fear of closeness, but it may just as well be a reflection of the therapist's anachronistic view of what constitutes proper analytic interactions. How is the patient to understand the analyst's intent if he or she, for instance, conveys a patient's need for responsiveness in an emotionally anemic manner? Even as we recognize issues of individuals' differing communicative styles, analysis remains an emotional cure for emotional ills.

The traditional reason, as is well known, for why analysts may be frightened to use a wider range of responsiveness is still connected to the fears of the consequences of gratification. Such analysts may be misled by a too narrow definition of what constitutes an analytic response and miss the specific meaning a patient needs us to understand and to be able to respond to. Critics of my views may object that I seem to be going to great lengths to build up a straw man that I can then tear down, that I may seem to describe psychoanalysis as a stuffy, rigid, and unemotional endeavor no longer reflected by contemporary clinical practice. If this is so, then I gladly stand corrected. Perhaps my difficulty—aside from when I am pointing out what I think are concrete instances of paradigmatic changes in psychoanalysis—lies in the fact that I am trying to describe therapeutic sensibilities that are often not so obviously visible or articulated but that are hidden in the nooks and crannies of historically permeated analytic traditions and attitudes—attitudes that nonetheless have an obsequious stranglehold on analytic conduct, to the detriment of both patient treatment and the practitioner by becoming a hindrance to the possibilities of utilizing the entire palette of the great variety of human emotional responsiveness. As I have tried to point out throughout this book, my intent is not to polemicize against traditional analytic views; rather, my intent is twofold: to demonstrate how the risks of relatedness dovetail with certain analytic premises and to offer an empathic articulation of these risks to free analysis from unnecessary restrictions. If the great endeavor of psychoanalysis, for which we are indebted to its founder, Freud, is to remain vital and be able to expand its tremendous potential, we must be as courageous as its founder was in questioning our methods.

Analysts may also fear joining the patient in acting out. As noted earlier, by replacing this term with that of enactment, we can avoid the criticism of being unanalytic. Analysts are now permitted to join the patient in enactments with the provision that we remain faithful to our traditional task of understanding the patient in the spirit of inquiry and with the goal of the unfolding and enhancement of the patient's inner world. Nonetheless, an air of stigmatization remains. In the sense that we often understand our patient's meanings and our own symbolic interpretations only much later, must we not then speak of our past interpretations as symbolic enactments? Thus, the necessity to dichotomize between symbolic and other forms of responses seems to collapse or at least become blurred in terms of clinical usefulness, in terms of their respective communicative value, and, in particular, as a guideline to what we consider a correct analytic response.

Being attuned to the level of structuralization and the specific meanings needing to be understood seems to be a more useful guide in choosing a form of response. Winnicott's idea that a good interpretation is experienced by the patient as a kind of holding could therefore also just as well be turned around. Holding the patient—be it by interpretation, some form of direct expression of feelings (such as an encouragement) or other types of provision, or some form of physical contact—can then also be understood as an accurate interpretation, if not in the narrow sense, and therefore as analytic. Analyzing means understanding—nothing more and nothing less—and understanding can be expressed in various forms of attuned responsiveness. In offering a patient an interpretation of how we understand him or her, we can therefore use as many modes as they did to convey their inner world to us. Accepting a present from a patient, giving him or her a kleenex, or reading a text outside the analytic hour that he or she has given us must then no longer necessarily be viewed as collusively acting out. Once again, our rule of thumb applies: we need to understand what each of these interactions means to the patient.

Conversely, to refuse a response on the level of enactment may deflate and shame the patient into renewed hiding, just at the point that he or she has mustered the courage to proudly show a new growth impulse. In the actions cited, even if the patient's actions entail defensive aspects, they are certainly also modes of attempting or soliciting contact and of showing him- or herself to us. The clinical benefit of verbalizing our understanding of the patient will then be context-dependent and left to the discretion of the therapist. Sometimes, less said is more on the road to cure.

Much progress has been made in what constitutes proper analytic responsiveness. It was, of course, Kohut's recognition that he wasn't addressing the issues his patients needed him to understand that led to a different kind of responsiveness. It was his conceptualization of the selfobject transference and selfobject interpretations that initiated the widening of the range of our responsiveness. Mirroring tentative states of selfhood is now recognized as necessary and supportive of enfeebled states of cohesiveness. Nonetheless, to this day, the view that supportive interactions, be it through selfobject interpretations, the recognition of the value of enactments and nonverbal interactions, or the addition of leading-edge interpretations to our psychoanalytic repertoire, is still seen as unanalytic. Recent discoveries in the neurosciences come to a different conclusion.[2] Thus, supportive interactions are recognized as the only form of response that reaches patients where the process of self- and object differentiation is in the foreground. Symbolized interpretations that address the patient as a separate object and that therefore bypass the supportive aspect of the selfobject function of the therapist do not reach such patients.

DISCUSSION OF THE CASE MATERIAL OF MRS. B

I would like to begin this discussion by stressing that the issue is not that the analyst *become* the perfect empathys' for the patient. Nor is it to attempt undoing or making up for the original developmental deficit. As stated in chapter 4, this is not possible. What we can do is offer alternatives, such as a form of relatedness in which new structures of subjectivity can develop or the opportunity of adding new experiences to our emotional memories, all of which will allow patients an expansion of their emotional worlds. We are not talking about replacing old organizing principles—as noted earlier, in times of stress, we may revert to old structures of organization. Rather, we are speaking of an expansion of the patients' horizons of experience. Through the repetition of new patterns of interaction with us, patients may be able to internalize new modes of caretaking toward themselves and come to different, more positive emotional conclusions about themselves and the nature of relatedness to others and therefore gain a more vital perspective on their place in the world.

Furthermore, the point is not that the analyst becomes the good object in an intentional role enactment of what he thinks the patient might need. "Hoffmann (1996) and Renik (1998) both propose that [it is] the spontaneous, authentic moments when the analyst breaks out of the confines of the technical, analytic ritual [that] are the key moments that bring about change" (Lichtenberg et al., 2002, p. 89). Lichtenberg et al. write about the clinical efficacy and benefit of "disciplined spontaneous engagements, that is, affective enactments of spontaneous communication by the analyst that emerge—erupt—within the structure of an analytic relationship" (p. 89). Insofar as intersubjectivity theory prefers practical wisdom to an adherence to technical rules and inasmuch as we would consider the emergence, even the eruptive emergence, as a product of the intersubjective field, we would say that while what emerges may surprise us, we would still not conceptualize it necessarily as a breaking out of the confines of the analytic process. We would also view spontaneous eruptions of affective communication as adhering to the inner logic of the intersubjective field, even if it is a logic that we understand only later.

The point I wish to make is that if we don't regard spontaneous, affective enactments as being radically different than other forms of analytic communication or responsiveness—such as patients' statements or therapist's interpretations on the symbolic level—then we can be more at ease in allowing such communications to occur. I realize that symbolization is a developmental milestone and that in an adult the inability to symbolize may be due either to the necessity to repress certain subjectively dangerous feelings or to certain feeling states that were never validated by the surround and that thus remain part of the unvalidated unconscious. In this sense, it remains important to differentiate between symbolized and enacted productions of our patients. But this clinically valuable differentiation should not be confused with a judgment about what constitutes a legitimate analytic communication or response. Rather, the differentiation pertains solely to the assessment of the psychological level we are dealing with.

Returning now to the discussion of Mrs. B, I would like to explore the central question of what was therapeutically curative. The therapeutic effect lies not only in my willingness to respond to her wishes but also in the effect that our ongoing dialogue and search of what it is like to be her, from moment to moment, had for her sense of existing.

Of course, as Mrs. B pointed out, the fact that I did agree to her wish for physical contact has been pivotal for her sense of healing. I did not agree because I had the illusion that this action could not possibly make up for a childhood devoid of a basic human need: quantitatively speaking, this would amount to the proverbial drop in the bucket. I agreed because Mrs. B allowed me to see that my responding to her wish was essential for her—essential on various levels. First, she had the courage to ask, thus pitting a lifetime of negative experience against the hope of one good experience, seemingly against all odds overcoming the fear of dreadful repetition. She was aware that I had had a body-psychotherapy training (biosynthesis), and while she knew that this had widened the scope of my understanding, she was also aware that it had not become an integral part of my daily practice. Thus, the request itself testifies to her new sense of entitlement and self-worth.

Second, it was essential for her to be able to regain a certain sense of basic trust, analogous to Winnicott's ([1951])1983) baby not needing to differentiate yet betweeen reaching for the object and the object being offered. "The mother makes it possible for the baby to have the illusion that the breast, and what the breast means, *has been created* by the impulse out of need" (p. 101). Here we can clearly see both the importance of the impulse arising in the patient and its being met: her seeking me and my letting myself be found. In the development of infants, Winnicott ([1945] 1983) described this as leading to a psychosomatic collusion that, in turn, leads to a sense of "I-am." Winnicott called psychosomatic collusion "personalisation," or the psyche indwelling in the soma. "Personalisation means not only that the psyche is placed in the body [but that] the whole of the body becomes the dwelling place of the self" (p. 41). In terms of a baby, the good-enough mother's adaptive behavior turns a "this is just what I needed" experience into an "I have created this" experience. Thus, for Mrs. B, a reintegration process between body and psyche began, just as a renewed hope developed that there is a link between inner and outer reality. Later she commented that "the aura that always separated me from people and the world has gone." The feeling that what was wanted was created and found to be there led to a belief "that the world can contain what is wanted and needed" (p. 44). If we recall that trauma robs us of our absolutisms, then the process of Mrs. B gives us reason to hope that therapy can to some extent compensate for such losses. Again, in her words, "The fact that I have loving feelings allows me to feel lovable."

Although there is usually not only one point of derailment in a person's development, for Mrs. B the rejection of her body selfhood and the need for physical attunement was compounded by the experiences of rape and physical abuse. So it seems that her entire treatment had gravitated toward this point, toward her wish for a benign, nonviolent, nonsexual physical contact, in the hope of amending her mind–body split and reconnecting to a basic feeling of belonging to the human race. In her own mind, this was the core issue that needed to be addressed and to be experienced in a new, healing way in order for her to move on. One can only imagine the devastating effect it would have had had I been unable to respond to her growth impulse, to her attempt at a developmental second chance. In hindsight, it reminds me of the sometimes highwire nature of our work underscoring the risks of relatedness. "The real challenge is to know the patient and, in doing so, provide what is essential: that solace that words, particularly for the more regressed patient, cannot provide" (Rudermann, 2000, p. 110).

I am neither saying that we are of necessity called on to always concretistically respond to our patients' wishes based on their deficits nor saying that to do so leads to the boundariless fulfillment of wishes. Boundaries—within ethical guidelines—are subjective and must be established by patient and therapist alike, on an individual basis, as a result of our understanding of the multiple intersubjective fields we find ourselves in. That is the beauty and, perhaps for some, as I have heard it expressed, the source of apprehensiveness and unease toward intersubjectivity theory because we can't know what will emerge and what will be called for. Nonetheless, the responsibilty clearly is the therapist's.

I have chosen a more extensive description of the analysis of Mrs. B because it highlights the intersubjective nature of the therapeutic process as well as the risks of relatedness for both the patient and the analyst. It also demonstrates the new, more balanced emphasis in psychoanalysis on working with the growth potential of patients. In this clinical example—which is somewhat unusual for an analysis (though not as unusual as is claimed[3]) in that it involved physical contact—psychological problems were ultimately being worked on at a highly significant symbolic level. In fact, it clearly shows how more archaic states become integrated in higher levels of structuralization. One recalls her moving statement that she now feels truly okay. The patient's need for touch symbolized on a very early level the need to be accepted and to feel lovable instead of feeling that her wishes were per se toxic and intolerable. She had felt that she was a burden that no other human being could respond to and therefore confirmed her conviction that life itself had rejected her. Another central fantasy she had was to shrink back to the size of an infant and lie on my chest. I can hardly imagine a more basic image of the human need to be accepted and to feel lovable.

TRANSFERENCE AND COUNTERTRANSFERENCE: THE INTERSUBJECTIVE FIELD

The case discussion would be incomplete without an exploration of my countertransference. I must preface this with some comments about how we understand countertransference. We refer to countertransference as all the ways that the analyst's structures of subjectivity organize the analytic relationship and, in particular, the patient's transference. In this regard, the countertransference, much like the transference, is seen as a psychological organizing activity. Thus, the same principles that inform our view of the transference apply to our view of the countertransference. We do not see it as a distortion, regression, displacement, or projection. We do, however, see it as shaping the patient's transference. Transference and countertransference are perfect examples of the intersubjective field. "Patient and analyst together form an indissoluble psychological system" (Atwood and Stolorow, 1984, p. 64). Orange (1995) introduced the concept of the cotransference to denote the analyst's contribution to the intersubjective field. In the broadest sense, cotransference therefore refers to the "concurrent and mutual organizing activity of analyst and patient" (p. 63). We prefer the term *cotransference* to *countertransference*, as it avoids the connotation of reacting against the transference as well as the implication that we could stand apart from the patient's experience "as if the countertransference were a bounded thing a clinician could use" (p. 67). Orange's concept concurs with Loewald's (1986) view that "it is ill-advised, indeed impossible, to treat transference and countertransference as separate issues. They are two faces of the same dynamic, rooted in the inextricable intertwinings with others" (p. 276 cited in in Orange, 1995, p. 67). "Cotransference treats the organizing activity of patient and analyst as two faces of the same dynamic. Neither activity needs a label with pejorative connotations" (Orange, 1995, p. 67). This does not mean, as stated before, that there are no differences in the participation of the analyst and the patient. The relationship is mutual but asymetrical. The cotransference includes both the personal history and the organizing principles of the analyst. Our knowledge of ourselves is indispensable for empathy in that we have to be able to realize the idiosyncratic nature of our perceptions in order to decenter from them and to be able to see what is different about the patient's subjective world. We "reserve the term countertransference for the analyst's delimited and reactive emotional memories that interfere with empathic understanding and optimal responsiveness" (p. 74). The criticism that may arise—that we have broadened the concept of countertransference to the extent of its becoming meaningless or, worse, as an expression of our narcissistic need to push ourselves into the foreground of the treament process—can hold true only if we do not accept the intersubjective nature of human existence in general and psychoanalysis in particular.

Now to my cotransference. A deeper analysis of my feelings led me to the uncomfortable truth that what I feared was not so much the force of her feelings but rather her feelings of deep affection. Why should such feelings be so frightening? I return to the theme of the risk of relatedness. Where there are feelings of love, fears of loss are never far behind. Love, it seems, is after all more frightening than aggression. Was I scared? Of course. But it also felt right to me. In retrospect, I asked myself what I was scared of. When Mrs. B surmised that she must be lovable because I put my hand on her head, I didn't contradict her. I use silence just as other analysts do: in order to remain an elusive presence and to give room for the patient's feelings and fantasies. I have feelings of fatherly affection for Mrs. B. Any parent knows the scope such feelings can have. I realized that my fear was related to not curtailing my feelings inwardly, that I somehow feared they could be without limits. I do not mean without limits in the sense that I might develop loving feelings, such as one has with a partner or wife, that would include a romantic/erotic component. While I have not been unaware of Mrs. B's appeal as a woman, this awareness is peripheral in comparison with the clarity of my awareness of her archaic needs for motherly attunement.

In this regard, my experiences with body psychotherapy were of great help to me. In many instances, physical contact, perhaps often feared for its possible sexual connotations, especially in psychoanalytic circles, actually brings forth the whole compexity of affective responses, demonstrating how much of sexual fantasy is actually a decontextualization of the many forms of the need for human contact. Ironically, sexual fantasies can also be indicative of a mind–body split, as the sexual fantasy will vanish when actual physical contact occurs. Along these lines, my first German analyst quipped that "sexuality is an invention of science." Self psychology has been criticized for a sexorectomy of psychoanalysis. In answer to this critique at a conference, Stolorow once humorously answered, "Is there sex after cohesion? You bet." The point we wish to make is that we do not ignore sexuality as a strong motivation in life. We object to its decontextualization, to the implicit neglect of its highly subjective meanings. Ian Suttie (1988) objected to what he called Freud's "pansexualism," which neglected the dimensions of tenderness. To reduce human strivings to sexuality—even in the broad sense that Freud did—and aggression is a narrowing of feelings that confuses a certain kind of peak experience in human emotion with the ability to feel the entire range and depth of emotion. Who is to say that a tender feeling cannot be as intense as a sexual feeling?

In the case of Mrs. B, I decided not to let fear stop the opening of the heart but to place my faith on the side of vulnerability and to allow for the risk of relatedness. This gave me a sense of calm, responsibility, cohesion, and gratitude. In essence, the goal of therapy is to get patients to love themselves and to remember who they are, and with any luck we might remember who we are. In describing the aims of psychoanalysis, Winnicott (1965) thought that therapists could work analytically with archaic levels of structuralization. "If our aim continues to be to verbalize the nascent conscious in terms of the transference, then we are practicing psychoanalysis; if not, then we are analysts practicing something else that we deem to be appropriate for the occasion. And why not?" (p. 170). The spirit of this quote still holds true. I would amend it by noting that, fortuitously, the field of psychoanalysis has not stood still and has expanded its thinking about what is appropriate for the occasion. To cite Kohut (1977), "Those who live in [the world of absolute values] are serious because their joyful search has ended—they have become defenders of the truth. . . . The world of creative science is inhabited by playful people who understand that the reality surrounding them is essentially unknowable" (pp. 206–207, cited in Rudermann, 2000, p. 122).

In her seminal article "Intimate Communications: The Values and Boundaries of Touch in the Psychoanalytic Setting," Ellen Rudermann (2000) makes several points that are germane to this discussion. She explains the role of touch in development and infant research. Touch plays a critical role in infant–caregiver bonding as well as in establishing a healthy self-image. She cites a number of authors[4] who "emphasized the sensory perceptive interchange between the infant and the caregiver and introduced a distinction between transference that is based on language and verbal symbols and that which is nonverbal" (p. 120). Nonverbal transference originating in the body is linked with preverbal experiences and, according to infant research, "can only be reached and reactivated via nonverbal channels—in particular through body language" (p. 120). As is well known, transference based on language and verbal symbols belongs to a later developmental stage. "Touch," she goes on to say, "need not be connected to sexuality or to aggressive behavior or be seen as a countertransferential acting out" (p. 120). Rather, in her experience, much as in mine, touch has a calming and soothing effect, especially with patients who suffer from basic feelings of defectiveness and worthlessness. Freud's idea, as I pointed out earlier, that blocking the discharge of the patient's instinctual drives—we would say blocking their nonverbal affective expressions—leads to their transformation into verbal symbolization has been found to be erroneous. Thus, the idea that nonverbal exchanges, including touch, impede the transference is now understood differently. With some patients, such as Mrs. B, the avoidance of physical contact would have amounted to a repetition of the original physical childhood rejection. In fact, the compliance with the taboo against touch may serve the resistance, reinforcing the cold, isolating idiom of care that the patient is so desparately trying to escape. Once again, the abstinent, neutral, and anonymous stance—as opposed to an interactive stance based on the spirit of inquiry—can be seen to create a therapeutic climate that unwittingly reproduces the very pathological situation it is trying to heal. Once again, lest I be misunderstood, I must stress the point that for some patients, it may be just as essential to employ a more low-key, reticent approach where the analyst's expressiveness is more restrained and not to use touch. However, this decision is based on the individual understanding of a particular patient and what he or she may need, not on a universally applicable idea of what constitutes the correct analytic stance. Thus, we are called on to question the internalization of abstinence as an "absolute" in psychoanalysis. In spite of this absolute, Rudermann also makes the point that Searles, Balint, and Winnicott employed physical contact in their work with some patients. With patients such as Mrs. B, we are called on to become "more resonant with the presexualized stage of touch—and comfortable with the nuances of developmental need, including touch" (McLaughlin, 1995, cited in Rudermann, 2000, pp. 112–113). It is our fear of the abuse of touching and not non-erotic touch itself that keeps us from being able to consider what may be the best response for a patient.

For Mrs. B, the fact that she was able to express the need to be touched meant a total revision of her most basic beliefs about herself and her life. As we were able to verbally reflect, on a symbolic level it implied that she could get what she needed, that she felt accepted, and that she was lovable. We were also working through the question of my emotional availability. So, while her neediness was profound and while she feared being overwhelmed by its extent as well as overwhelming me, if we understood that we were not dealing with an insatiable deficit but with a baby's need to be held with all the symbolic implications, we were able to diffuse any fears that accompany deep feelings. The analytic task remained the same: to understand what was needed, to respond to it, and then to put that understanding into words. As Winnicott taught us, the patient experiences a correct interpretation as if she were being held. And, as I have tried to explain, being held (or some form of touch) can also be seen as a correct interpretation—in the larger sense—of what a patient is expressing.

For me, as I came to understand, the fear was not to leave the symbolic trail of the spoken word or to get lost on the unspoken path of physical contact but to allow myself to feel. I didn't fear the touch; I feared being touched in the sense of moved, and this is the essence of the risk of relatedness in all our work. From the point of view of intersubjectivity theory, what was in essence determining the intersubjective field? Both feared nothing more than what I will call coming in from the cold. Our psychoanalytic encounter had given Mrs. B the "feeling of entering into a sunny lit room. I always thought that I was blind, but it was just dark where I used to be." She mentioned that she can now look at people with loving eyes. In body-psychotherapy terms, we might say that her eyes have become courageous. In analytic terms, we would say that by being able to reconnect to one human being (her analyst) in a profound way, she was simultaneously reconnecting to herself and the world. For psychotherapists, in the face of all the doubts concerning the value of psychotherapy, it is a comfort to know that one human being can make the difference and can deeply effect change in the life of another if we are willing to enter into the intersubjective field, to take the risk to walk the line and let the line walk us.

If we come full circle to the first image of the risk of relatedness and the game of 52-card pickup at the beginning of this book, both analyst and patient must see whether they are willing to enter into the risk of relatedness—sometimes a playful exchange, sometimes a frightening encounter, but hardly a game at all.

NOTES

1. A good example of this phenomenon can be found in Tilman Moser's (2004) discussion of his training analysis.
2. I am grateful to Dr. Fee Hintze for making this point in a lecture at the Arbeitsgemeinschaft für Psychoanalyse und Psychotherapie, 2006.
3. "It is unfortunate that some analysts, classical or otherwise, do not often write or reflect what they actually do in their sessions, but what they think their colleagues want to hear" (Rudermann, 2000, p. 109).
4. Ainsworth (1989); Beebe, Jaffe, and Lachmann (1992); Brazelton (1992); Lichtenberg et al. (1992); Mahler and McDevitt (1982); Main and Solomon (1990); Schore (1996); Stern (1985).

References

Ainsworth, M. D. (1989). Attachments beyond infancy. *American Psychologist* 4, 709–16.

Altmeyer, M. (2004). Self, narcissism and intersubjectivity. *Selbstpsychologie: Europäische Zeitschrift für Psychoanalytische Therapie und Forschung* 5, 275–88.

Aron, L. (1996). *A meeting of minds: Mutuality in psychoanalysis*. Hillsdale, NJ: Analytic Press.

Atwood, G. E., and Stolorow, R. D. (1979). *Faces in a cloud: Subjectivity in personality theory*. New York: Jason Aronson.

———. (1984). *Structures of subjectivity: Explorations in psychoanalytic phenomenology*. Hillsdale, NJ: Analytic Press.

Baranger, M., and Baranger, W. (1961/1962). La situacion analitica como campo dinamico. *Revista Uruguaya de Psicoanalisis* 4, 3–54.

Basch, M. (1985). Interpretation: Toward a developmental model. In A. Goldberg (ed.), *Progress in self psychology* (pp. 33–42). New York: Guilford Press.

Beebe, B., Jaffe, J., and Lachmann, F. M. (1992). A dyadic systems view of communication. In N. J. Skolnick and S. C. Warshaw (eds.), *Relational perspectives in psychoanalysis* (pp. 61–83). Hillsdale, NJ: Analytic Press.

Bergmann-Mausfeld, G. (2000). Empathie und Resonanz: Psychoanalyse und Säuglingsforschung. *Forum Psychoanalyse* 16, 204–13.

Bernstein, R. (1983). *Beyond objectivism and relativism: Science, hermeneutics, and praxis*. Philadelphia: University of Philadelphia Press.

Bettelheim, B. (1983). *Freud and man's soul*. New York: A. Knopf.

Bezoari, M., and Ferro, A. (1992). From a play between "parts" to transformations in the couple: Psychoanalysis in a bipersonal field. In L. N. Momigliano and A. Robutti (eds.), *Shared experience: The psychoanalytic dialogue* (pp. 43–65). London: Karnac Books.

Bion, W. (1990). *Brazilian lectures*. London: Karnac Books.

Bodansky, R. (2004). The benefit of humor in psychoanalysis. *Selbstpsychologie: Europäische Zeitschrift für Psychoanalytische Therapie und Forschung* 5, 298–310.

Bollas, C. (1987). *The shadow of the object: Psychoanalysis of the unthought known.* London: Free Association Books.

———. (1989). *Forces of destiny: Psychoanalysis and human idiom.* London: Free Association Books.

Brandchaft, B. (1993). To free the spirit from its cell. In R. D. Stolorow, G. Atwood, and B. Brandchaft (eds.), *The intersubjective perspective* (pp. 57–76). Northvale, NJ: Jason Aronson.

Brazelton, T. B. (1992). *Touchpoints: Your child's emotional and behavioral development.* Boston: Addison-Wesley.

Demos, E. V. (1987). Affect and the development of the self: A new frontier. In A. Goldberg (ed.), *Frontiers in self psychology* (pp. 27–53). Hillsdale, NJ: Analytic Press.

Dufresne, T. (2003). *Killing Freud: Twentieth-century culture and the death of psychoanalysis.* London: Continuum.

Emde, R., and Sorce, J. (1983). The rewards of infancy: Emotional availability and maternal referencing. In J. Call, E. Galenson, and R. Tyson (eds.), *Frontiers of Infant Psychiatry* (pp. 17–30). New York: Basic Books.

Freud, A. (1936). Das Ich und die Abwehrmechanismen. In *Die Schriften der Anna Freud* (vol. 1, pp. 193–355). Frankfurt am Main: Fischer.

Freud, S. (1895). *Project for a scientific psychology.* Standard edition 1: 294–387. London: Hogarth Press, 1950.

———. (1910). Über Psychoanalyse. *Gesammelte Werke* (vol. 8, pp. 1–60). London: Imago Publishing Co. Ltd.

———. (1912). Ratschläge für den Arzt bei der psychoanalytischen Behandlung. *Gesammelte Werke* (vol. 8, pp. 376–387). London: Imago Publishing Co. Ltd.

———. (1915a). Bemerkungen über die Übertragungsliebe. *Gesammelte Werke* (vol. 10, pp. 306–21).

———. (1915b). Das Unbewußte. *Gesammelte Werke* (vol. 10, pp. 264–303).

———. (1961a). The ego and the id. In J. Strachey, ed. and trans., *The standard edition of the complete psychological works of Sigmund Freud,* vol. 19, pp. 3–66. London: Hogarth Press. Original edition 1923.

Gadamer, H. (1990). *Wahrheit und Methode: Grundzüge einer philosophischen Hermeneutik.* Tübingen: Mohr.

———. (1991). *Truth and method,* 2nd ed. Trans. J. Weinsheimer and D. Marshall. New York: Crossroads. Original edition 1975.

Gedo, J. (1975). To Heinz Kohut: On his 60th birthday. *The Annual of Psychoanalysis* 3:313–22. New York: International Universities Press.

Gill, M. M. (1982). *Analysis of transference: Vol. 1. Theory and technique.* New York: International Universities Press.

———. (1983). The interpersonal paradigm and the degree of the therapist's involvement. *Contemporary Psychoanalysis,* 19, 200–37.

———. (1984). Psychoanalysis and psychotherapy: A revision. *International Review of Psychoanalysis,* 11, 161–80.

———. (1994). *Psychoanalysis in transition.* Hillsdale, NJ: Analytic Press.

Goldberg, A. (ed.). (1985). *Progress in self psychology.* New York: Guilford Press.

Heisterkamp, G. (2002). Basales Verstehen: Handlungsdialoge in Psychotherapie und Psychoanalyse. Stuttgart: Pfeiffer bei Klett-Cotta.

Hoffmann, I. Z. (1996). The intimate and ironic authority of the psychoanalyst's presence. *Psychoanalytic Quarterly*, 65, 102–36.

Jaenicke, C. (1993). Self psychology is not supportive psychotherapy: An answer to its critics. *Psychoanalytic Review*, 80, 253–64.

———. (1999). Die Evolution der Bezogenheit: Von Kohuts Selbstpsychologie zu Stolorows Intersubjektivitätstheorie. In E. Bartosch (ed.), *Wunden der Seele—Chancen der Heilung* (pp. 15–39). Wien: Verlag Neue Psychoanalyse Wien.

———. (2001). Diskussion von Joseph D. Lichtenbergs "Übertragung als Kommunikation: Die Sprache des Körpers." *Selbstpsychologie: Europäische Zeitschrift für Psychoanalytische Therapie und Forschung*, 2, 305–10.

———. (2002). Summary. Deconstructing the myth of the neutral analyst: An alternative view from intersubjective systems theory. *Selbstpsychologie: Europäische Zeitschrift für Psychoanalytische Therapie und Forschung*, 3, 206–9.

Jaenicke, C., and Milch, W. (2002). Epilogue. *Selbstpsychologie: Europäische Zeitschrift für Psychoanalytische Therapie und Forschung* 3, 264–66.

Kernberg, O. (1975). *Borderline conditions and pathological narcissism*. New York: Jason Aronson.

Klein, G. (1973). Two theories or one? *Bulletin of the Menninger Clinic* 37:102–32.

Knoblauch, S. (2000). *The musical edge of therapeutic dialogue*. Hillsdale, NJ: Analytic Press.

Kohut, H. (1959). Introspection, empathy, and psychoanalysis: An examination of the relationship between mode of observation and theory. In Paul H. Ornstein (ed.), *The search for the self* (vol. 1, pp. 205–32). Madison, CT: International Universities Press.

———. (1971). *The analysis of the self*. New York: International Universities Press.

———. (1977). *The restoration of the self*. Madison, CT: International Universities Press.

———. (1980). Reflections on advances in self psychology. In A. Goldberg (ed.), *Advances in self psychology* (pp. 473–554). Madison, CT: International Universities Press.

———. (1982). Introspection, empathy, and the semicircle of mental health. *International Journal of Psycho-Analysis* 63, 395–408.

———. (1984a). Introspection, empathy, and the semicircle of mental health. In J. Lichtenberg, M. Bornstein, and D. Silver (eds.), *Empathy I* (pp. 81–100). Hillsdale, NJ: The Analytic Press.

———. (1984b). *How does psychoanalysis cure?* A. Goldberg and P. Stepansky (eds.). Chicago: University of Chicago Press.

Krystal, H. (1988). *Integration and self-healing: Affect, trauma, alexithymia*. Hillsdale, NJ: Analytic Press.

Lachmann, F. (2003). *Humor, spontaneity and communication in the therapeutic process*. Paper presented at the ISIPSE Conference, Rome.

———. (2005). Die therapeutische Wirkung und der therapeutische Akteur. *Selbstpsychologie: Europäische Zeitschrift für Psychoanalytische Therapie und Forschung*, 21/22, 327–43.

Lichtenberg, J. (2005a). *Craft and spirit: A guide to the exploratory psychotherapies*. Hillsdale, NJ: Analytic Press.

———. (2005b). Was wir heutzutage über Veränderungen als Resultat von expliziter Kommunikation wissen und was wir über den Einfluss impliziter Kommunikation dazulernen. *Selbstpsychologie: Europäische Zeitschrift für Psychoanalytische Therapie und Forschung* 21/22, 300–314.

Lichtenberg, J., Lachmann, F. M., and Fosshage, J. (1992). *Self and motivational systems: Toward a theory of psychoanalytic technique*. Hillsdale, NJ: Analytic Press.

———. (2002). *A spirit of inquiry: Communication in psychoanalysis*. Hillsdale, NJ: Analytic Press.

Loewald, H. (1960). Perspectives on memory. In *Papers on psychoanalysis* (pp. 148–73). New Haven, CT: Yale University Press.

Loewald, H. W. (1986). Transference-countertransference. *Journal of the American Psychoanalytic Association*, 34, 275–87.

Maccio, D. V. (1992). Surviving, existing, living: reflections on the analyst's anxiety. In L. N. Momigliano and A. Robutti (eds.), *Shared experience: The psychoanalytic dialogue* (pp. 89–120). London: Karnac Books.

Mahler, M., and McDevitt, J. (1982). Thoughts on the emergence of self, with particular emphasis on the body self. *Journal of the American Psychoanalytic Association* 30, 827–48.

Main, M., and Solomon, M. (1990). Procedures for identifying infants' disorganized disoriented states during the Ainsworth strange situation. In A. Goldberg, D. Cicchetti, and M. Cummings (eds.), *Attachment in the pre-school years: Theory, research and intervention* (pp. 121–60). Chicago: University of Chicago Press.

McLaughlin, J. (1995). Touching limits in the analytic dialogue. *Psychoanalytic Quarterly* 64, 446.

Meotti, A., and Meotti, F. (1988). *Colpa e responsabilita: Un altro problema per il contotransfert e línterpretazione*. Lecture, 8. Kongress der Italienischen Psychoanalytischen Vereinigung, Sorrento.

Miller, A. (1979) *Prisoners of childhood*. New York: Basic Books, 1981.

———. (1990). *The untouched key: Tracing childhood trauma in creativity and destructiveness* (H. Hannum and H. Hannum, trans.). New York: Doubleday Anchor Books.

Miller, J. (1985). How Kohut actually worked. In A. Goldberg (ed.), *Progress in self psychology* (pp. 12–30). New York: Guilford Press.

Mitchell, S. (1988). *Relational concepts in psychoanalysis: An integration*. Cambridge, MA: Harvard University Press.

———. (1993). *Hope and dread in psychoanalysis*. New York: Basic Books.

Momigliano, L. N., and A. Robutti (eds.). (1992). *Shared experience: The psychoanalytic dialogue*. London: Karnac Books.

Moser, T. (2004). Bekenntnisse einer halb geheilten Seele: Psychotherapeutische Erinnerungen. Frankfurt am Main: Suhrkamp.

Nunberg, H. (1951). Transference and reality. *International Journal of Psycho-Analysis* 32, 1–9.

Orange, D. M. (1995). *Emotional understanding: Studies in psychoanalytic epistemology*. New York: Guilford Press.

———. (2002). There is no outside: Empathy and authenticity in psychoanalytic process. *Psychoanalytic Psychology* 19, 686–700.

Orange, D. M., Atwood, G. E., and Stolorow, R. D. (1997). *Intersubjktivität in der Psychoanalyse: Kontextualismus in der psychoanalytischen Praxis*. Frankfurt am Main: Brandes and Apsel.

Ornstein, A. (1974). The dread to repeat and the new beginning. *Annual of Psychoanalysis* 2, 231–48.

Peirce, C. (1931–1935). *The collected papers of Charles Sanders Peirce*. C. Hartshorn and P. Weiss (eds.). Cambridge, MA: Harvard University Press. Original ed. 1905.

Piaget, J. (1974). *The place of the sciences of man in the system of sciences*. New York: Harper & Row.

Putnam, H. (1990). *Realism with a human face*. Cambridge, MA: Harvard University Press.

Reik, T. (1954). *Listening with the third ear: The inner experience of a psychoanalyst*. New York: Farrar, Straus & Cudahy.

Renik, O. (1993). Analytic interaction: Conceptualizing technique in light of the analyst's irreducible subjectivity. *Psychoanalytic Quarterly* 62, 553–71.

———. (1998). Getting real in analysis. *Psychoanalytic Quarterly* 67, 566–93.

———. (2005). Lecture, Symposium des Münchner Forums für Neue Entwicklungen in der Psychoanalyse. Munich.

Rudermann, E. G. (2000). Intimate communications: The values and boundaries of touch in the psychoanalytic setting. *Psychoanalytic Inquiry* 20, 108–23.

Schore, A. N. (1996). *Affect regulation and the origin of the self*. Hillsdale, NJ: Lawrence Erlbaum Associates.

Schwaber, E. (1981). Empathy: A mode of analytic listening. *Psychoanalytic Inquiry* 1, 357–92.

———. (1983). Psychoanalytic listening and psychic reality. *International Review of Psycho-Analysis* 10, 379–92.

Searles, H. (1965). *Collected papers on schizophrenia and related subjects*. New York: International Universities Press.

———. (1979). The patient as the therapist to his analyst. In *Countertransference and related subjects* (pp. 380–459). New York: International Universities Press.

Silberner-Becker, N., and Amler, M. (2005). Leading edge: The search for a developmental promoting self-object relationship: Towards a theory and technique. *Self Psychology: European Journal for Psychoanalytic Therapy and Research* 20, 262–87.

Socarides, D., and Stolorow, R. D. (1984–1985). Affects and selfobjects. In R. D. Stolorow, B. Brandchaft, and G. E. Atwood (eds.), *Psychoanalytic treatment: An intersubjective approach* (pp. 66–87). Hillsdale, NJ: Analytic Press, 1987.

Spezzano, C. (1993). *Affect in psychoanalysis: A clinical synthesis*. Hillsdale, NJ: Analytic Press.

Stern, D. N. (1985). *The interpersonal world of the infant*. New York: Basic Books.

———. (2004). *The present moment in psychotherapy and everyday life*. New York: Norton.

Stolorow, R. D. (1976). Psychoanalytic reflections on client-centered therapy in the light of modern conceptions of narcissism. *Psychotherapy: Theory, Research and Practice* 13, 26–29.

———. (1985). Toward a pure psychology of inner conflict. In A. Goldberg (ed.), *Progress in self psychology* (pp. 193–202). New York: Guilford Press.

———. (1999). The phenomenology of trauma and the absolutisms of everyday life: A personal journey. *Psychoanalytic Psychology* 16, 464–68.

———. (2003). Trauma and temporality. *Psychoanalytic Psychology* 20, 158–61.

Stolorow, R. D., and Atwood, G. E. (1979). *Faces in a cloud: Subjectivity in personality theory*. New York: Jason Aronson.

———. (1992). *Contexts of being: The intersubjective foundations of psychological life*. Hillsdale, NJ: Analytic Press.

Stolorow, R. D., Atwood, G. E., and Brandchaft, B. (1994). *The intersubjective perspective*. New York: Jason Aronson.

Stolorow, R. D., Atwood, G. E., and Orange, D. M. (1999). Kohut and contextualism: Toward a post-Cartesian psychoanalytic process. *Psychoanalytic Psychology* 16, 380–88.

———. (2002). *Worlds of experience: Interweaving philosophical and clinical dimensions in psychoanalysis*. New York: Basic Books.

Stolorow, R. D., Brandchaft, B., and Atwood, G. E. (1987). *Psychoanalytic treatment*. Hillsdale, NJ: Analytic Press.

Stolorow, R. D., and Lachmann, F. M. (1980). *Psychoanalysis of developmental arrests: Theory and treatment*. New York: International Universities Press.

Stone, L. (1961). *The psychoanalytic situation*. Madison, CT: International Universities Press.

Strozier, C. B. (2001). *Heinz Kohut: The making of a psychoanalyst*. New York: Farrar, Straus & Giroux.

Suttie, I. (1988). *The origins of love and hate*. London: Routledge and Kegan Paul. Original edition 1935.

Tolpin, M. (2002). Doing psychoanalysis of normal development: Forward edge transferences. In A. Goldberg (ed.), *Progress in self psychology* (vol. 18, pp. 167–90). Hillsdale, NJ: Analytic Press.

———. (2004). *Understanding the total transference: Repetitions of pathology and remobilization of normal development*. Fingert Memorial Lecture, St. Louis.

Tolpin, M., and Tolpin, P. (1996). Preface. In P. Tolpin and M. Tolpin (eds.), *The Chicago Institute lectures* (pp. ix–xxii). Hillsdale, NJ: Analytic Press.

Wachtel, P. (1993). *Therapeutic communication*. New York: Guilford Press.

Waelder, R. (1936). Das Prinzip der multiplen Funktion—Bemerkungen zur Überdeterminierung. In *Ansichten der Psychoanalyse: Eine Bestandsaufnahme* (pp. 57–76). Stuttgart: Klett-Cotta.

Winnicott, D. W. (1945). Primitive emotional development. In *Through pediatrics to psychoanalysis: Collected papers*. New York: Basic Books, 1958.

———. (1983). Die primitive Gefühlsentwicklung. In *Von der Kinderheilkunde zur Psychoanalyse* (pp. 58–76). Frankfurt am Main: Fischer.

———. (1951). Transitional objects and transitional phenomena. In *Through pediatrics to psychoanalysis: Collected papers*. New York: Basic Books.

———. (1983) Übergangsobjekte und Übergangsphänomene. In *Von der Kinderheilkunde zur Psychoanalyse* (pp. 300–319). Frankfurt am Main: Fischer.

———. (1965). *The maturational processes and the facilitating environment*. New York: International Universities Press.

Index

About the Author

Chris Jaenicke is faculty member and training and supervising analyst at the Arbeitsgemeinschaft für Psychoanalyse und Psychotherapie and faculty member at the Institut für Psychotherapie, both in Berlin. He is editor and publisher of *Self Psychology: European Journal for Psychoanalytic Therapy and Research*. The author of numerous articles on intersubjectivity theory and self psychology, he lives and is in private practice in Berlin, Germany.